D0385317

THE DAYS ARE LONG,
BUT THE YEARS ARE SHORT.

This journal belongs to

WHY I KEEP A ONE-SENTENCE JOURNAL

Several years ago, I became alarmed by how little I remembered from my own past, so I looked for a realistic way to keep a colorful record of my life. Because keeping a proper journal seemed far too daunting, I decided instead to keep a one-sentence journal.

Every night, I write just one sentence. And now that I've kept my journal for several years, I know that one sentence is indeed enough to keep memories vivid. A one-sentence journal is very satisfying: it's manageable, so it doesn't feel like a burden; it gives me the feeling of accomplishment and growth that's so important to happiness; it helps me recall happy moments; and it gives me a reason to reflect on my experiences in a loving and grateful way.

We tend to overestimate what can be done in the short term, and underestimate what can be done in the long term, a little bit at a time. Writing one sentence a day sounds easy, and it is; at the end of the year, it adds up to a marvelous record.

—Gretchen Rubin, author of *The Happiness Project*

POTTER STYLE

Cover and Interior Designs
by Danielle Deschenes

Portions of this work are based on *The Happiness
Project* by Gretchen Rubin, copyright © 2009
by Gretchen Rubin. Published by Harper Collins
Publishers, New York, in 2009.

www.clarksonpotter.com

ISBN: 978-0-307-88857-0

Printed in China

JANUARY

1

What you do *every day* matters more
than what you do *once in a while*.

20 __ * _____
_____
_____

20 __ * _____
_____
_____

20 __ * _____
_____
_____

20 __ * _____
_____
_____

20 __ * _____
_____
_____

2

JANUARY

"The whole universe is change and life
itself is but what you deem it."

—*Marcus Aurelius*

20 __ * _____
_____
_____
_____

20 __ * _____
_____
_____
_____

20 __ * _____
_____
_____
_____

20 __ * _____
_____
_____
_____

20 __ * _____
_____
_____
_____

JANUARY

Happy people are more altruistic, more productive, more
helpful, more likable, more creative, more resilient, more
interested in others, friendlier, and healthier.

20 __ * _____

_____

_____

_____

20 __ * _____

_____

_____

_____

20 __ * _____

_____

_____

_____

20 __ * _____

_____

_____

_____

20 __ * _____

_____

_____

_____

4 JANUARY

Happiness is right here, right now—as in the 1908 play by Maurice Marterlinck, *The Blue Bird*, in which two children spend a year searching the world for the Blue Bird of Happiness, only to find it waiting for them when they finally return home.

20 ___ * _____

_____

_____

_____

20 ___ * _____

_____

_____

_____

20 ___ * _____

_____

_____

_____

20 ___ * _____

_____

_____

_____

20 ___ * _____

_____

_____

_____

JANUARY

When life is taking its ordinary course, it's hard to remember what matters. If you want a happiness project, you have to *make* the time.

20 __ * _____

_____

_____

_____

20 __ * _____

_____

_____

_____

20 __ * _____

_____

_____

_____

20 __ * _____

_____

_____

_____

20 __ * _____

_____

_____

_____

6 JANUARY

"We do not learn so much by our successes as we learn by failures—our own and others'. Especially if we see the failures properly corrected."

—*Frank Lloyd Wright*

20 __ * _____

_____

_____

_____

20 __ * _____

_____

_____

_____

20 __ * _____

_____

_____

_____

20 __ * _____

_____

_____

_____

20 __ * _____

_____

_____

_____

JANUARY

7

"So we must exercise ourselves in the things which bring happiness, since, if that be present, we have everything, and, if that be absent, all our actions are directed toward attaining it."

—*Epicurus*

20 __ *_____

_____

_____

_____

20 __ *_____

_____

_____

_____

20 __ *_____

_____

_____

_____

20 __ *_____

_____

_____

_____

20 __ *_____

_____

_____

_____

JANUARY

Aim to live so that you don't look back, at the end of your life or after some great catastrophe, and think, "How happy I was then, if only I'd realized it!"

20 __ * _____

_____

_____

_____

20 __ * _____

_____

_____

_____

20 __ * _____

_____

_____

_____

20 __ * _____

_____

_____

_____

20 __ * _____

_____

_____

_____

JANUARY

By doing a little bit each day, you can get
a lot accomplished.

20 __ * _____
_____
_____
_____

20 __ * _____
_____
_____
_____

20 __ * _____
_____
_____
_____

20 __ * _____
_____
_____
_____

20 __ * _____
_____
_____
_____

JANUARY

Don't let the perfect be the enemy of the good.

20 __ * _____

_____

_____

_____

20 __ * _____

_____

_____

_____

20 __ * _____

_____

_____

_____

20 __ * _____

_____

_____

_____

20 __ * _____

_____

_____

_____

JANUARY

Sometimes strengths can be weaknesses, and weaknesses
can be strengths.

20 __ *_____

_____

_____

_____

20 __ *_____

_____

_____

_____

20 __ *_____

_____

_____

20 __ *_____

_____

_____

_____

20 __ *_____

_____

_____

_____

JANUARY

"When the student is ready, the teacher appears."

—*Buddhist saying*

20 __ * _____

_____

_____

_____

20 __ * _____

_____

_____

_____

20 __ * _____

_____

_____

_____

20 __ * _____

_____

_____

_____

20 __ * _____

_____

_____

_____

JANUARY

Happiness is contagious. Happy people make people happy.

20 __ * _____

_____

_____

20 __ * _____

_____

_____

20 __ * _____

_____

_____

20 __ * _____

_____

_____

20 __ * _____

_____

_____

JANUARY

Happiness—which can seem like a complex, lofty, and intangible goal—is quite influenced by simple factors like getting enough sleep and exercise.

20 __ * _____
_____
_____
_____

20 __ * _____
_____
_____
_____

20 __ * _____
_____
_____
_____

20 __ * _____
_____
_____
_____

20 __ * _____
_____
_____
_____

JANUARY

Turn off the light. It's all too easy to stay up to read,
answer e-mails, watch TV, pay bills, or putter, instead of
going to bed. Resolve to get enough sleep.

20 __ *_____

_____

_____

_____

20 __ *_____

_____

_____

_____

20 __ *_____

_____

_____

_____

20 __ *_____

_____

_____

_____

20 __ *_____

_____

_____

_____

16 JANUARY

Make time for play. What is play?—an activity that's satis-fying, has no economic significance, doesn't create social harm, and doesn't necessarily lead to praise or recognition.

20 __ * _____

_____

_____

_____

20 __ * _____

_____

_____

_____

20 __ * _____

_____

_____

_____

20 __ * _____

_____

_____

_____

20 __ * _____

_____

_____

_____

JANUARY

17

"Nothing great was ever achieved without enthusiasm."

—*Ralph Waldo Emerson*

20 __ * _____
_____
_____
_____

20 __ * _____
_____
_____
_____

20 __ * _____
_____
_____
_____

20 __ * _____
_____
_____
_____

20 __ * _____
_____
_____
_____

18   JANUARY

One effective way to judge whether a particular
course of action will make you happy in the future is
to ask people currently following that course of action
if they're happy with it—and assume that you'll
probably feel the same way.

20 __ * _____

_____

_____

_____

20 __ * _____

_____

_____

_____

20 __ * _____

_____

_____

_____

20 __ * _____

_____

_____

_____

20 __ * _____

_____

_____

_____

JANUARY

You can choose what you do;
you can't choose what you *like* to do.

20 __ * _____
_____
_____
_____

20 __ * _____
_____
_____
_____

20 __ * _____
_____
_____
_____

20 __ * _____
_____
_____
_____

20 __ * _____
_____
_____
_____

JANUARY

The opposite of *happiness* is *unhappiness*, not *depression*. Depression is a grave condition that requires urgent attention. But even people who aren't depressed can benefit from trying to be happier.

20 __ * _____

_____

_____

_____

20 __ * _____

_____

_____

_____

20 __ * _____

_____

_____

_____

20 __ * _____

_____

_____

_____

20 __ * _____

_____

_____

_____

JANUARY

Identify the problem. Stating a problem clearly
often suggests its solution.

20 __ * _____

_____

_____

_____

20 __ * _____

_____

_____

_____

20 __ * _____

_____

_____

_____

20 __ * _____

_____

_____

_____

20 __ * _____

_____

_____

_____

JANUARY

Follow the "one-minute rule": don't postpone any task that can be done in less than one minute. Put away your umbrella, file a document—such steps take only moments, but the cumulative impact is impressive.

20 __ * _____

_____

_____

_____

20 __ * _____

_____

_____

_____

20 __ * _____

_____

_____

_____

20 __ * _____

_____

_____

_____

20 __ * _____

_____

_____

_____

JANUARY

One of life's small pleasures is to return something to its proper place; returning the shoe polish to the closet's second shelf gives the archer's satisfaction of hitting a mark.

20 __ * _____

_____

_____

_____

20 __ * _____

_____

_____

_____

20 __ * _____

_____

_____

_____

20 __ * _____

_____

_____

_____

20 __ * _____

_____

_____

_____

JANUARY

"Happiness, not in another place but this place,
not for another hour but this hour."

—*Walt Whitman*

20 ___ * _____
_____
_____
_____

20 ___ * _____
_____
_____
_____

20 ___ * _____
_____
_____
_____

20 ___ * _____
_____
_____
_____

20 ___ * _____
_____
_____
_____

JANUARY

Look for ways to keep mornings running smoothly;
the morning sets the tone for everyone's days.

20 __ * _____

_____

_____

20 __ * _____

_____

_____

20 __ * _____

_____

_____

20 __ * _____

_____

_____

20 __ * _____

_____

_____

JANUARY

"Reframe" a particular chore by choosing to enjoy it. "I hate making the bed." "No, I *love* making the bed!"

20 __ * _____

_____

_____

_____

20 __ * _____

_____

_____

_____

20 __ * _____

_____

_____

_____

20 __ * _____

_____

_____

_____

20 __ * _____

_____

_____

_____

JANUARY

"A lifetime can well be spent correcting and improving one's own faults without bothering about others."

—*Edward Weston*

20 __ * _____

_____

_____

_____

20 __ * _____

_____

_____

_____

20 __ * _____

_____

_____

_____

20 __ * _____

_____

_____

_____

20 __ * _____

_____

_____

_____

JANUARY

Buddhists talk about "skillful" and "unskillful" emotions, and this has the right connotation of effort and competence. People assume that a person who *acts* happy must *feel* happy, but although it's in the very nature of happiness to seem effortless and spontaneous, it often takes great skill.

20 __ * _____

_____

_____

_____

20 __ * _____

_____

_____

_____

20 __ * _____

_____

_____

_____

20 __ * _____

_____

_____

_____

20 __ * _____

_____

_____

_____

JANUARY

"No man is happy who does not think himself so."

—*Publilius Syrus*

20 __ * _____

_____

_____

20 __ * _____

_____

_____

20 __ * _____

_____

_____

20 __ * _____

_____

_____

20 __ * _____

_____

_____

30 JANUARY

One of the best ways to make yourself happy is to make other people happy. Be selfless, if only for selfish reasons.

20 __ * _____

_____

_____

_____

20 __ * _____

_____

_____

_____

20 __ * _____

_____

_____

_____

20 __ * _____

_____

_____

_____

20 __ * _____

_____

_____

_____

JANUARY

"It is easy to be heavy: hard to be light."

— *G. K. Chesterton*

20 __ * _____

_____

_____

_____

20 __ * _____

_____

_____

_____

20 __ * _____

_____

_____

_____

20 __ * _____

_____

_____

_____

20 __ * _____

_____

_____

_____

1 FEBRUARY

"When one loves, one does not calculate."

— St. Thérèse of Lisieux

20 __ * _____
_____
_____
_____

20 __ * _____
_____
_____
_____

20 __ * _____
_____
_____
_____

20 __ * _____
_____
_____
_____

20 __ * _____
_____
_____
_____

FEBRUARY

To "spend out" is to give up keeping score,
to give love without calculation.

20 __ * _____

_____

_____

20 __ * _____

_____

_____

20 __ * _____

_____

_____

20 __ * _____

_____

_____

20 __ * _____

_____

_____

3 FEBRUARY

It's far more gratifying to act in a loving way than
to act in a dismissive or argumentative way.

20 __ * _____

_____

_____

_____

20 __ * _____

_____

_____

_____

20 __ * _____

_____

_____

_____

20 __ * _____

_____

_____

_____

20 __ * _____

_____

_____

_____

FEBRUARY

"Kindness in words creates confidence.
Kindness in thinking creates profoundness.
Kindness in giving creates love."

—Lao Tzu

20 __ * _____

_____

_____

20 __ * _____

_____

_____

20 __ * _____

_____

_____

20 __ * _____

_____

_____

20 __ * _____

_____

_____

FEBRUARY

"Perhaps it is the simplest and most popular truths that are also the deepest after all."

— Thomas Merton

20 __ * _____

_____

_____

_____

20 __ * _____

_____

_____

_____

20 __ * _____

_____

_____

_____

20 __ * _____

_____

_____

_____

20 __ * _____

_____

_____

_____

FEBRUARY

The things that go wrong often make the best memories.

20 __ * _____

_____

_____

_____

20 __ * _____

_____

_____

_____

20 __ * _____

_____

_____

_____

20 __ * _____

_____

_____

20 __ * _____

_____

_____

_____

FEBRUARY

Spread family cheer. Share happy news and funny incidents with your friends and family.

20 __ * _____
_____
_____
_____

20 __ * _____
_____
_____
_____

20 __ * _____
_____
_____
_____

20 __ * _____
_____
_____
_____

20 __ * _____
_____
_____
_____

FEBRUARY

Any single happy experience may be amplified
or minimized, depending on how much attention
is focused on it.

20 __ * _____

_____

_____

_____

20 __ * _____

_____

_____

_____

20 __ * _____

_____

_____

_____

20 __ * _____

_____

_____

_____

20 __ * _____

_____

_____

_____

FEBRUARY

Because of "emotional contagion," we unconsciously catch emotions from other people—whether good moods or bad moods. Aim to infect others with good cheer.

20 __ * _____
_____
_____
_____

20 __ * _____
_____
_____
_____

20 __ * _____
_____
_____
_____

20 __ * _____
_____
_____
_____

20 __ * _____
_____
_____
_____

FEBRUARY 10

"You can never predict what little things in the way somebody looks or talks or acts will set off peculiar emotional reactions in other people."

—*Andy Warhol*

20 __ * _____

_____

_____

_____

20 __ * _____

_____

_____

_____

20 __ * _____

_____

_____

_____

20 __ * _____

_____

_____

20 __ * _____

_____

_____

_____

11

FEBRUARY

"For a crowd is not company, and faces are but a
gallery of pictures, and talk but a tinkling cymbal,
where there is no love."

—*Francis Bacon*

20 __ * _____

_____

_____

_____

20 __ * _____

_____

_____

_____

20 __ * _____

_____

_____

_____

20 __ * _____

_____

_____

_____

20 __ * _____

_____

_____

_____

FEBRUARY

Everyone from contemporary scientists to ancient philosophers agrees that having strong social ties is probably the most meaningful contributor to happiness. Make time for the people who are important to you.

20 __ * _____

_____

_____

_____

20 __ * _____

_____

_____

_____

20 __ * _____

_____

_____

_____

20 __ * _____

_____

_____

_____

20 __ * _____

_____

_____

_____

FEBRUARY

Unsurprisingly, people are much more likely to feel close to a family member who often expresses affection than one who rarely does.

20 __ * _____

_____

_____

_____

20 __ * _____

_____

_____

_____

20 __ * _____

_____

_____

_____

20 __ * _____

_____

_____

_____

20 __ * _____

_____

_____

_____

FEBRUARY

"I know of no other way to perfection but love."

—*St. Thérèse of Lisieux*

20 __ * _____

_____

_____

_____

20 __ * _____

_____

_____

_____

20 __ * _____

_____

_____

_____

20 __ * _____

_____

_____

_____

20 __ * _____

_____

_____

_____

15   **FEBRUARY**

Bring people together. Make an introduction,
arrange a blind date, give a reference, take steps
to help people get to know each other.

20 __ * _____
_____
_____
_____

20 __ * _____
_____
_____
_____

20 __ * _____
_____
_____
_____

20 __ * _____
_____
_____
_____

20 __ * _____
_____
_____
_____

FEBRUARY 16

"Of all the things that wisdom provides to help one live one's entire life in happiness, the greatest by far is the possession of friendship."

—*Epicurus*

20 __ * _____

_____

_____

_____

20 __ * _____

_____

_____

_____

20 __ * _____

_____

_____

_____

20 __ * _____

_____

_____

_____

20 __ * _____

_____

_____

_____

FEBRUARY

Remember birthdays. Sending out birthday e-mails or
letters ensures that you'll be in touch with a friend at
least once a year.

20 ___ * _____

_____

_____

_____

20 ___ * _____

_____

_____

_____

20 ___ * _____

_____

_____

_____

20 ___ * _____

_____

_____

_____

20 ___ * _____

_____

_____

_____

FEBRUARY 18

"Any time that is not spent on love is wasted."

—*Tasso*

20 ___ * _____

20 ___ * _____

20 ___ * _____

20 ___ * _____

20 ___ * _____

FEBRUARY

Mindfulness is the cultivation of conscious, nonjudgmental awareness. Of its many benefits, mindfulness helps you stay in the present moment.

20 __ * _____

_____

_____

_____

20 __ * _____

_____

_____

_____

20 __ * _____

_____

_____

_____

20 __ * _____

_____

_____

_____

20 __ * _____

_____

_____

_____

FEBRUARY

"It is by studying little things that we attain the great art of having as little misery, and as much happiness, as possible."

— *Samuel Johnson*

20 __ * _____

_____

_____

_____

20 __ * _____

_____

_____

_____

20 __ * _____

_____

_____

_____

20 __ * _____

_____

_____

_____

20 __ * _____

_____

_____

_____

FEBRUARY

Stimulate the mind in new ways. Tackling unfamiliar
challenges enhances your experience of the present
moment and your awareness of yourself.

20 __ * _____
_____
_____
_____

20 __ * _____
_____
_____

20 __ * _____
_____
_____

20 __ * _____
_____
_____
_____

20 __ * _____
_____
_____
_____

FEBRUARY

Use your time efficiently, yet make time to wander,
to play, to go off the path.

20 __ * _____
_____
_____

20 __ * _____
_____
_____

20 __ * _____
_____
_____

20 __ * _____
_____
_____

20 __ * _____
_____
_____

FEBRUARY

"Live in each season as it passes; breathe the air, drink the drink, taste the fruit, and resign yourself to the influences of each."

—*Henry David Thoreau*

20 __ * _____
_____
_____
_____

20 __ * _____
_____
_____
_____

20 __ * _____
_____
_____
_____

20 __ * _____
_____
_____
_____

20 __ * _____
_____
_____
_____

FEBRUARY

Passion is a critical factor in professional success. People who love their work bring an intensity and enthusiasm that's impossible to match through sheer diligence.

20 __ * _____

_____

_____

_____

20 __ * _____

_____

_____

_____

20 __ * _____

_____

_____

_____

20 __ * _____

_____

_____

_____

20 __ * _____

_____

_____

_____

FEBRUARY

If you're pursuing a challenging goal, gather people around you who share your interest and can give you support and encouragement.

20 ___ * _____

_____

_____

_____

20 ___ * _____

_____

_____

_____

20 ___ * _____

_____

_____

_____

20 ___ * _____

_____

_____

_____

20 ___ * _____

_____

_____

_____

FEBRUARY

Finding ways to make your office more pleasant will help you work more effectively. Something as simple as a potted plant can improve the atmosphere.

20 __ * _____

_____

_____

20 __ * _____

_____

_____

20 __ * _____

_____

_____

20 __ * _____

_____

_____

20 __ * _____

_____

_____

_____

FEBRUARY

"People do best what comes naturally."

—*John F. Kennedy*

20 __ * _____

_____

_____

_____

20 __ * _____

_____

_____

_____

20 __ * _____

_____

_____

_____

20 __ * _____

_____

_____

_____

20 __ * _____

_____

_____

_____

FEBRUARY 28

Although people assume they prefer to have many choices, in fact, facing too many choices can be discouraging. In some situations, having fewer options makes people happier.

20 __ * _____

_____

_____

_____

20 __ * _____

_____

_____

_____

20 __ * _____

_____

_____

_____

20 __ * _____

_____

_____

_____

20 __ * _____

_____

_____

_____

29 FEBRUARY

"Between the ages of twenty and forty we are engaged in the process of discovering who we are, which involves learning the difference between accidental limitations which it is our duty to outgrow, and the necessary limitations of our nature beyond which we cannot trespass without impunity."

—W. H. Auden

20 __ * _____

_____

_____

_____

20 __ * _____

_____

_____

_____

20 __ * _____

_____

_____

_____

20 __ * _____

_____

_____

_____

20 __ * _____

_____

_____

_____

MARCH

1

What do *you* want? If you don't want something,
getting it won't make you happy.

20 __ * _____

_____

_____

20 __ * _____

_____

_____

20 __ * _____

_____

_____

20 __ * _____

_____

_____

20 __ * _____

_____

_____

MARCH

Merely making and sticking to a decision is a source
of happiness, because this action gives you a feeling of
control, of efficacy, of responsibility.

20 __ * _____

20 __ * _____

20 __ * _____

20 __ * _____

20 __ * _____

MARCH

"Happiness is essentially a state of going
somewhere wholeheartedly, one-directionally,
without regret or reservation."

—*W. H. Sheldon*

0 __ * _____

_____

_____

_____

0 __ * _____

_____

_____

_____

0 __ * _____

_____

_____

_____

0 __ * _____

_____

_____

_____

0 __ * _____

_____

_____

_____

4 MARCH

To be happy, think about *feeling good*, *feeling bad*,
and *feeling right*, in an *atmosphere of growth*.

20 __ * _____

_____

_____

20 __ * _____

_____

_____

20 __ * _____

_____

_____

20 __ * _____

_____

_____

20 __ * _____

_____

_____

MARCH

"Happiness is neither virtue nor pleasure nor
this thing nor that, but simply growth.
We are happy when we are growing."

—*William Butler Yeats*

20 ⬜ * _____

_____

_____

_____

20 ⬜ * _____

_____

_____

_____

20 ⬜ * _____

_____

_____

_____

20 ⬜ * _____

_____

_____

_____

20 ⬜ * _____

_____

_____

_____

6 MARCH

"Feeling right" is about living the life that's right for you in occupation, location, family situation, and other circumstances. It's also about virtue: doing your duty, behaving rightly, living up to the expectations you set for yourself.

20 __ * _____
_____
_____
_____

20 __ * _____
_____
_____
_____

20 __ * _____
_____
_____
_____

20 __ * _____
_____
_____
_____

20 __ * _____
_____
_____
_____

MARCH

7

You can change your life without changing your life
by finding more happiness in your own kitchen.

20 __ * _____

_____

_____

20 __ * _____

_____

_____

20 __ * _____

_____

_____

20 __ * _____

_____

_____

20 __ * _____

_____

_____

MARCH

Keeping a chart can be an important tool to help boost happiness. People are more likely to make progress on goals that are broken into concrete, measurable actions with some kind of structured accountability and positive reinforcement.

20 __ * _____

_____

_____

20 __ * _____

_____

_____

20 __ * _____

_____

_____

20 __ * _____

_____

_____

20 __ * _____

_____

_____

MARCH

If you're feeling overwhelmed or worried, go for a walk or wash some dishes. Repetitive activities trigger the body's relaxation response and so help to reduce stress.

20 __ * _____

20 __ * _____

0 __ * _____

0 __ * _____

0 __ * _____

10 MARCH

"Whoever is happy will make others happy, too."

—*Anne Frank*

20 __ * _____
_____
_____
_____

20 __ * _____
_____
_____
_____

20 __ * _____
_____
_____
_____

20 __ * _____
_____
_____
_____

20 __ * _____
_____
_____
_____

MARCH

11

Challenging yourself to learn something new brings happiness because it allows you to expand your self-definition. You become larger.

20 __ * _____

_____

_____

20 __ * _____

_____

_____

20 __ * _____

_____

_____

_____

20 __ * _____

_____

_____

20 __ * _____

_____

_____

_____

MARCH

In order to have more success, be willing to accept more failure. If you're not failing, you're not trying hard enough.

20 __ * _____
_____
_____
_____

20 __ * _____
_____
_____
_____

20 __ * _____
_____
_____
_____

20 __ * _____
_____
_____
_____

20 __ * _____
_____
_____
_____

MARCH

"Ah, but a man's reach should exceed his grasp,
or what's a heaven for?"

—*Robert Browning*

20 __ * _____

_____

_____

20 __ * _____

_____

_____

20 __ * _____

_____

_____

20 __ * _____

_____

_____

20 __ * _____

_____

_____

14   MARCH

Some happiness might be called "fog happiness." Fog is elusive. Fog surrounds you and transforms the atmosphere but when you try to examine it, it vanishes. Fog happiness is the kind of happiness you get from activities that, examined closely, don't really seem to bring much happiness at all—yet somehow they do.

20 __ * _____

_____

_____

_____

20 __ * _____

_____

_____

_____

20 __ * _____

_____

_____

_____

20 __ * _____

_____

_____

_____

20 __ * _____

_____

_____

_____

MARCH

15

"Though we travel the world over to find the beautiful,
we must carry it with us or we find it not."

—*Ralph Waldo Emerson*

20 __ * _____

_____

_____

_____

20 __ * _____

_____

_____

_____

20 __ * _____

_____

_____

_____

20 __ * _____

_____

_____

_____

20 __ * _____

_____

_____

_____

16

MARCH

People are very adaptable and quickly adjust to
a new life circumstance—for better or worse.

20 ___ * _____

_____

_____

_____

20 ___ * _____

_____

_____

_____

20 ___ * _____

_____

_____

_____

20 ___ * _____

_____

_____

_____

20 ___ * _____

_____

_____

_____

MARCH 17

"Happiness and misery consist in a progression towards better or worse; it does not matter how high up or low down you are, it depends not on this, but on the direction in which you are tending."

—*Samuel Butler*

20 __ * _____

_____

_____

_____

20 __ * _____

_____

_____

_____

20 __ * _____

_____

_____

_____

20 __ * _____

_____

_____

_____

20 __ * _____

_____

_____

_____

18   MARCH

Beware of the hedonic treadmill, which makes it easy to grow accustomed to pleasures and advances, such as a new car or new job title. Too soon, that good feeling wears off.

20 __ * _____
_____
_____
_____

20 __ * _____
_____
_____
_____

20 __ * _____
_____
_____
_____

20 __ * _____
_____
_____
_____

20 __ * _____
_____
_____
_____

MARCH

"The chief happiness for a man is to be what he is."

—*Erasmus*

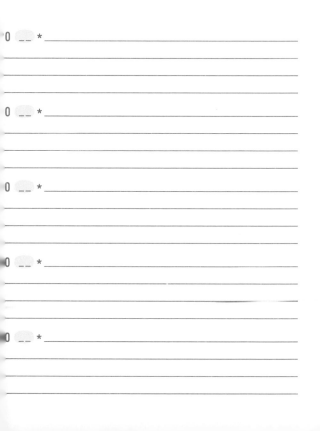

0 __ * _____

_____

_____

_____

0 __ * _____

_____

_____

_____

0 __ * _____

_____

_____

_____

0 __ * _____

_____

_____

_____

_____

0 __ * _____

_____

_____

_____

20 MARCH

Radical happiness projects, such as Henry David Thoreau's move to Walden Pond, can be exhilarating—the fresh start, the total commitment, the leap into the unknown. But you don't have to reject your life in order to be happier.

20 ___ * _____

_____

_____

_____

20 ___ * _____

_____

_____

_____

20 ___ * _____

_____

_____

_____

20 ___ * _____

_____

_____

_____

20 ___ * _____

_____

_____

_____

MARCH

What's fun for other people may not be fun for you—
and vice versa. Acknowledge what you enjoy,
not what you *wish* you enjoyed.

20 __ * _____

20 __ * _____

20 __ * _____

20 __ * _____

20 __ * _____

MARCH

Exercising is an effective way to snap out of a funk. Even
a quick, ten-minute walk provides an immediate energy
boost and improves mood.

20 __ * _____
_____
_____

20 __ * _____
_____
_____

20 __ * _____
_____
_____

20 __ * _____
_____
_____

20 __ * _____
_____
_____
_____

MARCH

"All truly great thoughts are conceived while walking."

—Nietzsche

20 __ * _____

_____

_____

_____

20 __ * _____

_____

_____

_____

20 __ * _____

_____

_____

_____

20 __ * _____

_____

_____

_____

20 __ * _____

_____

_____

_____

MARCH

Act the way you want to feel. By acting *as if* you feel more energetic, you can *become* more energetic.

20 __ * _____

_____

_____

_____

20 __ * _____

_____

_____

_____

20 __ * _____

_____

_____

_____

20 __ * _____

_____

_____

_____

20 __ * _____

_____

_____

_____

MARCH

To become more energetic, tackle both the *physical* and *mental* aspects of energy: get enough sleep, get some exercise, clear off your desk, get rid of the junk in your car.

20 __ * _____

_____

_____

20 __ * _____

_____

_____

20 __ * _____

_____

_____

20 __ * _____

_____

_____

20 __ * _____

_____

_____

26 MARCH

"Men are disturbed not by things, but by
the view they take of them."

—*Epictetus*

20 __ * _____

_____

_____

_____

20 __ * _____

_____

_____

_____

20 __ * _____

_____

_____

_____

20 __ * _____

_____

_____

_____

20 __ * _____

_____

_____

_____

MARCH

You can't change anyone else—as tempting as it is to try.
You can only change yourself.

20 __ * _____

20 __ * _____

20 __ * _____

20 __ * _____

20 __ * _____

MARCH

The absence of *feeling bad* isn't enough to make you feel happy; you must strive to find sources of *feeling good*.

20 ___ * _____

_____

_____

_____

20 ___ * _____

_____

_____

_____

20 ___ * _____

_____

_____

_____

20 ___ * _____

_____

_____

_____

20 ___ * _____

_____

_____

_____

MARCH

"Happiness is in the taste, and not in the things themselves; we are happy from possessing what we like, not
from possessing what others like."

— *La Rochefoucauld*

20 __ * _____

_____

_____

_____

20 __ * _____

_____

_____

_____

20 __ * _____

_____

_____

_____

20 __ * _____

_____

_____

_____

20 __ * _____

_____

_____

_____

30 MARCH

If something is really fun for you, you'll look forward to it; find it energizing, not draining; and you won't feel guilty about it later.

20 __ * _____

_____

_____

_____

20 __ * _____

_____

_____

_____

20 __ * _____

_____

_____

_____

20 __ * _____

_____

_____

_____

20 __ * _____

_____

_____

_____

MARCH

"The least strained and most natural ways
of the soul are the most beautiful; the best
occupations are the least forced."

—*Michel de Montaigne*

20 __ * _____

_____

_____

_____

20 __ * _____

_____

_____

_____

20 __ * _____

_____

_____

_____

20 __ * _____

_____

_____

_____

20 __ * _____

_____

_____

_____

1 APRIL

"If we had no winter, the spring would not be so pleasant;
if we did not taste of adversity, prosperity would not
be so welcome."

—Anne Bradstreet

20 __ * _____

_____

_____

20 __ * _____

_____

_____

20 __ * _____

_____

_____

20 __ * _____

_____

_____

20 __ * _____

_____

_____

APRIL

Make a list, do a little each day, and stay calm. Nothing is nsurmountable if you do what you know ought to be done, little by little.

0 ___ * _____

0 ___ * _____

0 ___ * _____

0 ___ * _____

0 ___ * _____

3 APRIL

"Our greatest weariness comes from work not done."

—Eric Hoffer

20 __ * _____

_____

_____

_____

20 __ * _____

_____

_____

_____

20 __ * _____

_____

_____

_____

20 __ * _____

_____

_____

_____

20 __ * _____

_____

_____

_____

APRIL

Sometimes the most difficult part of doing a task is just deciding to *do* it.

) ___ *_____

_____

_____

_____

) ___ *_____

_____

_____

_____

) ___ *_____

_____

_____

_____

) ___ *_____

_____

_____

_____

) ___ *_____

_____

_____

_____

5

APRIL

"No money is better spent than what is laid out for domestic satisfaction."

—*Samuel Johnson*

20 __ * _____

_____

_____

_____

20 __ * _____

_____

_____

_____

20 __ * _____

_____

_____

_____

20 __ * _____

_____

_____

_____

20 __ * _____

_____

_____

_____

APRIL

6

If you can't find something, clean up.

20 __ * _____
_____
_____
_____

20 __ * _____
_____
_____
_____

20 __ * _____
_____
_____
_____

20 __ * _____
_____
_____
_____
_____

20 __ * _____
_____
_____
_____

7 APRIL

Somewhere, keep an empty shelf. An empty shelf means possibility; space to expand; a luxurious waste of something useful for the sheer elegance of it.

20 __ * _____

_____

_____

_____

20 __ * _____

_____

_____

_____

20 __ * _____

_____

_____

_____

20 __ * _____

_____

_____

_____

20 __ * _____

_____

_____

_____

APRIL

"In the long run men hit only what they aim at. Therefore, though they should fail immediately, they had better aim at something high."

—*Henry David Thoreau*

20 __ * _____

_____

_____

_____

20 __ * _____

_____

_____

_____

20 __ * _____

_____

_____

_____

20 __ * _____

_____

_____

_____

20 __ * _____

_____

_____

_____

APRIL

Follow the "evening tidy-up rule": take ten minutes before bed to do simple tidying. This calming nightly habit helps prepare you for sleep and makes mornings more serene and pleasant.

20 ___ * _____
_____
_____
_____

20 ___ * _____
_____
_____
_____

20 ___ * _____
_____
_____
_____

20 ___ * _____
_____
_____
_____

20 ___ * _____
_____
_____
_____

APRIL

10

Singing in the morning is a quick way to set a cheerful mood for the day.

0 __ * _____

_____

_____

0 __ * _____

_____

_____

0 __ * _____

_____

_____

0 __ * _____

_____

_____

0 __ * _____

_____

_____

11 APRIL

"For the love of God and my Sisters (so charitable toward me) I take care to appear happy and especially *to be so*."

—*St. Thérèse of Lisieux*

20 __ * _____

_____

_____

_____

20 __ * _____

_____

_____

_____

20 __ * _____

_____

_____

_____

20 __ * _____

_____

_____

_____

20 __ * _____

_____

_____

_____

APRIL

It takes energy, generosity, and
discipline to be lighthearted.

20 ___ * _____

_____

_____

_____

20 ___ * _____

_____

_____

_____

20 ___ * _____

_____

_____

_____

20 ___ * _____

_____

_____

_____

20 ___ * _____

_____

_____

_____

APRIL

"Whoever is merry and cheerful has always a good reason
for so being, namely the very fact that he is so."

— Schopenhauer

20 __ * _____

_____

_____

_____

20 __ * _____

_____

_____

_____

20 __ * _____

_____

_____

_____

20 __ * _____

_____

_____

_____

20 __ * _____

_____

_____

_____

APRIL

14

Look for reasons to find things funny, to laugh out loud, and to appreciate other people's humor.

0 __ * _____

_____

_____

_____

0 __ * _____

_____

_____

_____

0 __ * _____

_____

_____

_____

0 __ * _____

_____

_____

_____

0 __ * _____

_____

_____

_____

APRIL

Laugh at *yourself*. Try not to take yourself too seriously.

20 __ * _____
_____
_____
_____

20 __ * _____
_____
_____
_____

20 __ * _____
_____
_____
_____

20 __ * _____
_____
_____
_____

20 __ * _____
_____
_____
_____

APRIL

Question the "true rules" you apply during your day, such as "Meetings are a waste of time" or "I'm too busy." Instead of applying them unthinkingly, use them only when they guide you to decisions that reflect your true priorities.

___ _____

_____

_____

_____

___ _____

_____

_____

_____

___ _____

_____

_____

_____

___ _____

_____

_____

_____

___ _____

_____

_____

_____

APRIL

"It is neither wealth nor splendor, but tranquillity and occupation, which give happiness."

—*Thomas Jefferson*

20 __ * _____

_____

_____

_____

20 __ * _____

_____

_____

_____

20 __ * _____

_____

_____

_____

20 __ * _____

_____

_____

_____

20 __ * _____

_____

_____

_____

APRIL

Money alone can't buy happiness. But used wisely, money can buy things that contribute mightily to happiness.

20 __ * _____

20 __ * _____

20 __ * _____

20 __ * _____

20 __ * _____

APRIL

"Everybody has to make up their mind if money is money
or if money isn't money and sooner or later they always do
decide that money is money."

—*Gertrude Stein*

20 __ * _____

_____

_____

_____

20 __ * _____

_____

_____

_____

20 __ * _____

_____

_____

_____

20 __ * _____

_____

_____

_____

20 __ * _____

_____

_____

_____

APRIL

Look for ways to spend money to support your happiness
goals, such as staying close to family and friends,
promoting energy and health, working more efficiently,
and eliminating sources of boredom and irritation.

20 __ * _____

_____

_____

_____

20 __ * _____

_____

_____

_____

20 __ * _____

_____

_____

_____

20 __ * _____

_____

_____

_____

20 __ * _____

_____

_____

_____

21 APRIL

Happiness theory suggests that if you buy a pair of boots or a kitchen table, you'll soon become accustomed to the new possession and be no happier than you were before. Nevertheless, many people make purchases for the fleeting jolt of happiness they get from the very act of gain.

20 __ * _____

_____

_____

_____

20 __ * _____

_____

_____

_____

20 __ * _____

_____

_____

_____

20 __ * _____

_____

_____

_____

20 __ * _____

_____

_____

_____

APRIL

22

"A multitude of small delights constitute happiness."

—*Charles Baudelaire*

___ * _____

___ * _____

___ * _____

___ * _____

___ * _____

APRIL

"A man is not only happy but wise also, if he is trying, during his lifetime, to be the sort of man he wants to be found at his death."

— *Thomas à Kempis*

20 __ * _____

_____

_____

_____

20 __ * _____

_____

_____

_____

20 __ * _____

_____

_____

_____

20 __ * _____

_____

_____

_____

20 __ * _____

_____

_____

_____

APRIL

24

The days are long, but the years are short.

0 ___ * _____

_____

_____

_____

0 ___ * _____

_____

_____

_____

0 ___ * _____

_____

_____

_____

0 ___ * _____

_____

_____

_____

0 ___ * _____

_____

_____

_____

APRIL

"Contemplate the extent and stability of the heavens, and then at last cease to admire worthless things."

—Boethius

20 __ * _____

_____

_____

_____

20 __ * _____

_____

_____

_____

20 __ * _____

_____

_____

_____

20 __ * _____

_____

_____

_____

20 __ * _____

_____

_____

_____

APRIL

Take time to steer your mind toward the transcendent and the timeless, away from the immediate and the shallow. Appreciate the glories of the present moment and ordinary life.

20 __ * _____

_____

_____

_____

20 __ * _____

_____

_____

_____

20 __ * _____

_____

_____

_____

20 __ * _____

_____

_____

_____

20 __ * _____

_____

_____

_____

27 APRIL

"Of all mindfulness meditations, that on death is supreme."

—*Buddha*

20 __ * _____

_____

_____

_____

20 __ * _____

_____

_____

_____

20 __ * _____

_____

_____

_____

20 __ * _____

_____

_____

_____

20 __ * _____

_____

_____

_____

APRIL

Appreciate the obedience of your body—
the simple ability to eat or walk or hear.

0 __ * _____
_____
_____
_____

0 __ * _____
_____
_____
_____

0 __ * _____
_____
_____
_____

0 __ * _____
_____
_____
_____

0 __ * _____
_____
_____
_____

29 **APRIL**

Gratitude is a key to happiness. Consistently grateful people are happier and more satisfied with their lives.

20 __ * _____

_____

_____

20 __ * _____

_____

_____

20 __ * _____

_____

_____

20 __ * _____

_____

_____

20 __ * _____

_____

_____

APRIL

"Pleasing yourself is not so easy.
It can even seem frightening."

—*Christopher Alexander*

20 __ * _____

0 __ * _____

0 __ * _____

0 __ * _____

0 __ * _____

1

MAY

"There is, indeed, something inexpressibly pleasing in the annual renovation of the world, and the new display of the treasures of nature."

—*Samuel Johnson*

20 __ * _____

_____

_____

_____

20 __ * _____

_____

_____

_____

20 __ * _____

_____

_____

_____

20 __ * _____

_____

_____

_____

20 __ * _____

_____

_____

_____

MAY

Remind yourself of all the reasons you have to be grateful.

20 __ * _____

_____

_____

_____

20 __ * _____

_____

_____

20 __ * _____

_____

_____

_____

20 __ * _____

_____

_____

20 __ * _____

_____

_____

_____

MAY

To gain a feeling of detachment and calm,
contemplate the beauty of nature.

20 ___ * _____

_____

_____

_____

20 ___ * _____

_____

_____

_____

20 ___ * _____

_____

_____

_____

20 ___ * _____

_____

_____

_____

20 ___ * _____

_____

_____

_____

MAY

"You will find something more in woods than in books.
Trees and stones will teach you that which you can never
learn from masters."

—*St. Bernard*

) ⸻ * _____

_____

_____

_____

) ⸻ * _____

_____

_____

_____

) ⸻ * _____

_____

_____

_____

) ⸻ * _____

_____

_____

_____

⸻ * _____

_____

_____

_____

MAY

Gratitude brings freedom from envy.

20 __ * _____

_____

_____

_____

20 __ * _____

_____

_____

_____

20 __ * _____

_____

_____

_____

20 __ * _____

_____

_____

_____

20 __ * _____

_____

_____

_____

MAY

One of the most universal spiritual practices is the imitation of a spiritual master as a way to gain understanding and discipline. Identify *your* spiritual master.

__ * _____

_____

_____

__ * _____

_____

_____

_____

__ * _____

_____

_____

_____

__ * _____

_____

_____

_____

__ * _____

_____

_____

_____

7 MAY

Practice the Zen art of meditating on a "koan" —
a statement that can't be grasped by reason or explained
in words. "What was your face before your parents were
born?" Meditating on koans promotes mindful thinking
because their meaning can't be comprehended with
familiar, conventional logic.

20 __ * _____

_____

_____

_____

20 __ * _____

_____

_____

_____

20 __ * _____

_____

_____

_____

20 __ * _____

_____

_____

_____

20 __ * _____

_____

_____

_____

MAY

"Carpenters fashion wood; fletchers fashion arrows;
the wise fashion themselves."

—Buddha

0 ___ * _____

_____

_____

_____

0 ___ * _____

_____

_____

_____

0 ___ * _____

_____

_____

0 ___ * _____

_____

_____

_____

0 ___ * _____

_____

_____

_____

MAY

Eat better, eat less, exercise more.

20 __ * _____

_____

_____

20 __ * _____

_____

_____

20 __ * _____

_____

_____

20 __ * _____

_____

_____

20 __ * _____

_____

_____

MAY

10

"Man loves company even if it is only that of a small burning candle."

— *Georg Christoph Lichtenberg*

11

MAY

Keeping a food diary is an effective way to encourage
yourself to eat more healthfully.

20 __ * _____

_____

_____

_____

20 __ * _____

_____

_____

_____

20 __ * _____

_____

_____

_____

20 __ * _____

_____

_____

_____

20 __ * _____

_____

_____

_____

MAY

"How few there are who have courage enough to own their Faults, or resolution enough to mend them!"

—*Benjamin Franklin*

0 __ * _____
_____
_____
_____

0 __ * _____
_____
_____
_____

0 __ * _____
_____
_____
_____

) __ * _____
_____
_____
_____

) __ * _____
_____
_____
_____

MAY

"We are what we repeatedly do. Excellence, then,
is not an act, but a habit."

—Aristotle

20 __ * _____

_____

_____

_____

20 __ * _____

_____

_____

_____

20 __ * _____

_____

_____

_____

20 __ * _____

_____

_____

_____

20 __ * _____

_____

_____

_____

MAY

To change your feelings, change your actions. A "fake it till you feel it" strategy may sound hokey, but it is extremely effective.

20 __ * _____
_____
_____
_____

20 __ * _____
_____
_____
_____

20 __ * _____
_____
_____
_____

20 __ * _____
_____
_____
_____

20 __ * _____
_____
_____
_____

MAY

"One is not always happy when one is good; but one is always good when one is happy."

—*Oscar Wilde*

20 __ *_____

_____

_____

_____

20 __ *_____

_____

_____

_____

20 __ *_____

_____

_____

_____

20 __ *_____

_____

_____

_____

20 __ *_____

_____

_____

_____

MAY

Happiness has a particularly strong influence in a relationship because partners pick up each other's moods so easily.

20 __ * _____

20 __ * _____

20 __ * _____

20 __ * _____

20 __ * _____

MAY

"Holding on to anger is like grasping a hot coal with the intent of throwing it at someone else; you are the one who gets burned."

—*Buddha*

20 __ * _____

_____

_____

_____

20 __ * _____

_____

_____

_____

20 __ * _____

_____

_____

_____

20 __ * _____

_____

_____

_____

20 __ * _____

_____

_____

_____

MAY

It's tempting to tell people, "There's no reason to worry," "Don't be scared," or "You'll see, you'll have fun." But denying others' bad feelings intensifies them; acknowledging their bad feelings allows their good feelings to return.

0 ___ * _____

_____

_____

_____

0 ___ * _____

_____

_____

_____

0 ___ * _____

_____

_____

_____

0 ___ * _____

_____

_____

_____

0 ___ * _____

_____

_____

_____

MAY

Aggressively expressing anger doesn't relieve anger but rather amplifies it. On the other hand, not expressing anger often allows it to disappear without leaving ugly traces.

20 ⬤ * _____

_____

_____

_____

20 ⬤ * _____

_____

_____

_____

20 ⬤ * _____

_____

_____

_____

20 ⬤ * _____

_____

_____

_____

20 ⬤ * _____

_____

_____

_____

MAY

"Reject your sense of injury, and the injury
itself disappears."

—*Marcus Aurelius*

0 ___ * _____

_____

_____

_____

0 ___ * _____

_____

_____

_____

0 ___ * _____

_____

_____

_____

0 ___ * _____

_____

_____

_____

0 ___ * _____

_____

_____

_____

MAY

Fighting style is very important to the health of a
relationship. Try to fight right, to joke and be
affectionate even while disagreeing.

20 __ * _____

_____

_____

_____

20 __ * _____

_____

_____

_____

20 __ * _____

_____

_____

_____

20 __ * _____

_____

_____

_____

20 __ * _____

_____

_____

_____

MAY

22

"Action and feeling go together; and by regulating the action, which is under the more direct control of the will, we can indirectly regulate the feeling."

—*William James*

0 __ * _____

_____

_____

_____

0 __ * _____

_____

_____

_____

0 __ * _____

_____

_____

_____

0 __ * _____

_____

_____

_____

0 __ * _____

_____

_____

_____

MAY

It's easier to feel happy, and to behave yourself,
when you make the effort to stay physically comfortable—
by dressing appropriately, getting enough sleep,
managing pain, and the like.

20 __ * _____

_____

_____

_____

20 __ * _____

_____

_____

_____

20 __ * _____

_____

_____

_____

20 __ * _____

_____

_____

_____

20 __ * _____

_____

_____

_____

MAY

"Everything should be made as simple
as possible, but not simpler."

—*Albert Einstein*

) ⬭ * _____
_____
_____
_____

) ⬭ * _____
_____
_____
_____

) ⬭ * _____
_____
_____
_____

) ⬭ * _____
_____
_____
_____

) ⬭ * _____
_____
_____
_____

MAY

The resolution to laugh out loud goes beyond mere laughter. Responding with laughter sometimes means that you have to give up your pride, your defensiveness, your self-centeredness.

20 __ * _____

_____

_____

20 __ * _____

_____

_____

20 __ * _____

_____

_____

20 __ * _____

_____

_____

20 __ * _____

_____

_____

MAY

"We don't laugh because we're happy—
we're happy because we laugh."

—*William James*

0 😊 *_____

_____

_____

_____

0 😊 *_____

_____

_____

_____

0 😊 *_____

_____

_____

_____

0 😊 *_____

_____

_____

_____

0 😊 *_____

_____

_____

_____

MAY

"I have found that most people are about as happy as they make up their minds to be."

—*Abraham Lincoln*

20 __ * _____

_____

_____

_____

20 __ * _____

_____

_____

_____

20 __ * _____

_____

_____

_____

20 __ * _____

_____

_____

_____

20 __ * _____

_____

_____

_____

MAY

Quit nagging. Nothing kills good feelings between people more than nagging. Anyway, nagging doesn't work.

0 ___ *_____

_____

_____

0 ___ *_____

_____

_____

_____

0 ___ *_____

_____

_____

_____

0 ___ *_____

_____

_____

_____

0 ___ *_____

_____

_____

_____

MAY

No dumping. Hearing someone complain is tiresome whether you're in a good or bad mood, and whether or not the complaining is justified.

20 __ * _____

_____

_____

_____

20 __ * _____

_____

_____

_____

20 __ * _____

_____

_____

_____

20 __ * _____

_____

_____

_____

20 __ * _____

_____

_____

_____

MAY

30

"To hear complaints is wearisome alike to
the wretched and the happy."

— *Samuel Johnson*

0 __ * _____

0 __ * _____

0 __ * _____

0 __ * _____

0 __ * _____

MAY

"Not every end is a goal. A melody's end is not its goal;
nevertheless, so long as the melody has not reached its
end, it also has not reached its goal. A parable."

—*Nietzsche*

20 __ * _____
_____
_____
_____

20 __ * _____
_____
_____
_____

20 __ * _____
_____
_____
_____

20 __ * _____
_____
_____
_____

20 __ * _____
_____
_____
_____

JUNE

1

Be serious about play. Though having fun sounds
simple, it isn't. Think about how to shape your time
to get the most enjoyment from it.

0 __ * _____

_____

_____

_____

0 __ * _____

_____

_____

_____

0 __ * _____

_____

_____

_____

0 __ * _____

_____

_____

_____

0 __ * _____

_____

_____

_____

JUNE

2

"I was nearly forty before I felt how stupid it was to pretend to know things that I did not know and I still often catch myself doing so."

—*Samuel Butler*

20 __ * _____

_____

_____

_____

20 __ * _____

_____

_____

_____

20 __ * _____

_____

_____

_____

20 __ * _____

_____

_____

_____

20 __ * _____

_____

_____

_____

JUNE

Turning from one chore to another can make you feel trapped and drained, but fun is exhilarating. Taking the time to do something truly fun will make you better able to tackle your to-do list.

0 ___ * _____
_____
_____
_____

0 ___ * _____
_____
_____
_____

0 ___ * _____
_____
_____
_____

0 ___ * _____
_____
_____
_____

0 ___ * _____
_____
_____
_____

JUNE

"Everything turns out to be valuable that one does for one's self without thought of profit."

— *Marguerite Yourcenar*

20 __ * _____

_____

_____

_____

20 __ * _____

_____

_____

_____

20 __ * _____

_____

_____

_____

20 __ * _____

_____

_____

_____

20 __ * _____

_____

_____

_____

JUNE

5

Enthusiasm is more important to mastery than innate ability, because the single most important element in developing an expertise is the willingness to practice.

__ * _____

__ * _____

__ * _____

__ * _____

__ * _____

JUNE

Surprise stimulates the mind; successfully dealing with an unexpected situation gives a powerful sense of satisfaction

20 __ * _____
_____
_____
_____

20 __ * _____
_____
_____
_____

20 __ * _____
_____
_____
_____

20 __ * _____
_____
_____
_____

20 __ * _____
_____
_____
_____

JUNE

"Now and then it's good to pause in our
pursuit of happiness and just be happy."

—*Guillaume Appollinaire*

) ⬭ * _____

_____

_____

) ⬭ * _____

_____

_____

_____

) ⬭ * _____

_____

_____

) ⬭ * _____

_____

_____

) ⬭ * _____

_____

_____

JUNE

If you do new things—visit a museum for the first time, learn a new game, travel to a new place, meet new people— you're more apt to feel happy than a person who sticks to more familiar activities.

20 ___ * _____

_____

_____

_____

20 ___ * _____

_____

_____

_____

20 ___ * _____

_____

_____

_____

20 ___ * _____

_____

_____

_____

20 ___ * _____

_____

_____

_____

JUNE

"The great thing in this world is not so much where we
stand as in what direction we are moving."

—*Oliver Wendell Holmes Sr.*

0 __ * _____

_____

_____

_____

0 __ * _____

_____

_____

_____

0 __ * _____

_____

_____

_____

0 __ * _____

_____

_____

_____

0 __ * _____

_____

_____

_____

JUNE

It's easy to fall into the belief that when you arrive at a certain destination, you'll be happy. But arrival rarely makes us as happy as we anticipate.

20 __ * _____

_____

_____

_____

20 __ * _____

_____

_____

_____

20 __ * _____

_____

_____

_____

20 __ * _____

_____

_____

_____

20 __ * _____

_____

_____

_____

JUNE

11

The fun part doesn't come later, *now* is the fun part.

JUNE

Happiness depends partly on external circumstances, and it also depends on how you view those circumstances.

20 __ * _____

_____

_____

20 __ * _____

_____

_____

20 __ * _____

_____

_____

20 __ * _____

_____

_____

20 __ * _____

_____

_____

JUNE

> "Happiness and misery depend as much on
> temperament as on fortune."

> —*La Rochefoucauld*

20 __ * _____
_____
_____
_____

20 __ * _____
_____
_____
_____

20 __ * _____
_____
_____
_____

20 __ * _____
_____
_____
_____

20 __ * _____
_____
_____
_____

14 JUNE

"Choose what is best, and habit will make it pleasant and easy."

—*Plutarch*

20 __ * _____
_____
_____
_____

20 __ * _____
_____
_____
_____

20 __ * _____
_____
_____
_____

20 __ * _____
_____
_____
_____

20 __ * _____
_____
_____
_____

JUNE

An admittedly challenging but extremely effective way to ease a situation is to make a joke.

0 ⌣ *_____

_____

_____

_____

0 ⌣ *_____

_____

_____

_____

0 ⌣ *_____

_____

_____

_____

0 ⌣ *_____

_____

_____

_____

0 ⌣ *_____

_____

_____

_____

JUNE

Acknowledge the reality of people's feelings: Don't deny feelings such as anger, irritation, fear, or reluctance; instead, articulate the feeling and the point of view.

20 __ * _____
_____
_____
_____

20 __ * _____
_____
_____
_____

20 __ * _____
_____
_____
_____

20 __ * _____
_____
_____
_____

20 __ * _____
_____
_____
_____

JUNE 17

"If you make it a habit not to blame others, you will feel the growth of the ability to love in your soul, and you will see the growth of goodness in your life."

—Leo Tolstoy

0 __ * _____

_____

_____

0 __ * _____

_____

_____

0 __ * _____

_____

_____

0 __ * _____

_____

_____

0 __ * _____

_____

_____

JUNE

Try to be more observant and appreciative of the things that others do. We're far more aware of what *we* do than what other people do.

20 __ * _____

_____

_____

_____

20 __ * _____

_____

_____

_____

20 __ * _____

_____

_____

_____

20 __ * _____

_____

_____

_____

20 __ * _____

_____

_____

_____

JUNE

Beauty is no quality in things themselves: It exists merely in the mind which contemplates them."

— *David Hume*

0 ⸺ * _____

_____

_____

_____

0 ⸺ * _____

_____

_____

_____

0 ⸺ * _____

_____

_____

_____

0 ⸺ * _____

_____

_____

_____

0 ⸺ * _____

_____

_____

_____

JUNE

Cut people slack. Lives are far more complicated
than they appear from the outside.

20 __ * _____

_____

_____

20 __ * _____

_____

_____

20 __ * _____

_____

_____

20 __ * _____

_____

_____

20 __ * _____

_____

_____

JUNE

"From fifteen to eighteen is an age at which one is very
sensitive to the sins of others, as I know from recollections
of myself. At that age you don't look for what is hidden.
It is a sign of maturity not to be scandalized and to try to
find explanations in charity."

—Flannery O'Conner

____ * _____

_____

_____

_____

____ * _____

_____

_____

_____

____ * _____

_____

_____

_____

____ * _____

_____

_____

_____

____ * _____

_____

_____

_____

JUNE

"I will speak ill of no man and speak all the
good I know of everybody."

—*Benjamin Franklin*

20 __ * _____

_____

_____

_____

20 __ * _____

_____

_____

_____

20 __ * _____

_____

_____

_____

20 __ * _____

_____

_____

_____

20 __ * _____

_____

_____

_____

JUNE

Although gossip serves an important social function,
and it's certainly fun, it's not *nice*.

 * _____

_____
_____
_____
_____

 * _____

_____
_____
_____
_____

 * _____

_____
_____
_____

 * _____

_____
_____
_____

 * _____

_____
_____
_____

24 JUNE

Try not to judge people harshly, especially on your first meeting. Their actions might not reveal their enduring character but instead reflect some situation in which they find themselves.

20 ___ * _____

_____

_____

_____

20 ___ * _____

_____

_____

_____

20 ___ * _____

_____

_____

_____

20 ___ * _____

_____

_____

_____

20 ___ * _____

_____

_____

_____

JUNE 25

"It is almost a definition of a gentleman to say
that he is one who never inflicts pain."

—*John Henry Newman*

JUNE

In "spontaneous trait transference," what you say about *other people* sticks to you—even when you talk to someone who already knows you. So you do well to say only good things.

20 __ * _____

_____

_____

_____

20 __ * _____

_____

_____

_____

20 __ * _____

_____

_____

_____

20 __ * _____

_____

_____

_____

20 __ * _____

_____

_____

_____

JUNE

27

"I have often regretted my speech, never my silence."

—*Publilius Syrus*

0 __ * _____
_____
_____
_____

0 __ * _____
_____
_____
_____

0 __ * _____
_____
_____
_____

0 __ * _____
_____
_____
_____

0 __ * _____
_____
_____
_____

JUNE

"Associate with people who are likely to improve you."

—*Seneca*

20 __ * _____
_____
_____
_____

20 __ * _____
_____
_____
_____

20 __ * _____
_____
_____
_____

20 __ * _____
_____
_____
_____

20 __ * _____
_____
_____
_____

JUNE

Healthy self-esteem is a consequence of estimable actions.
If you're feeling bad about yourself, try doing something
worthy of your own respect.

⬤ __ * _____
_____
_____
_____

⬤ __ * _____
_____
_____
_____

⬤ __ * _____
_____
_____
_____

⬤ __ * _____
_____
_____
_____

⬤ __ * _____
_____
_____
_____

JUNE

Find ways to shower people with small treats and courtesies, praise, and appreciation. Small, frequent gestures of thoughtfulness are more important than candy on Valentine's Day.

20 __ * _____

_____

_____

20 __ * _____

_____

_____

20 __ * _____

_____

_____

20 __ * _____

_____

_____

20 __ * _____

_____

_____

JULY

1

All too often, what's *important* gets pushed aside while we deal with what's *urgent*. Make sure that your life reflects your real priorities.

20 __ * _____

_____

_____

_____

20 __ * _____

_____

_____

_____

20 __ * _____

_____

_____

_____

20 __ * _____

_____

_____

_____

20 __ * _____

_____

_____

_____

JULY

"If a man does not make new acquaintance as he advances
through life, he will soon find himself alone. A man should
keep his friendship in constant repair."

—*Samuel Johnson*

20 __ * _____

_____

_____

_____

20 __ * _____

_____

_____

_____

20 __ * _____

_____

_____

_____

20 __ * _____

_____

_____

_____

20 __ * _____

_____

_____

_____

JULY

3

Generous acts strengthen bonds of friendship.
Happiness is often boosted more by *giving*
support than from *receiving* support.

0 ___ * _____
_____
_____
_____

0 ___ * _____
_____
_____
_____

0 ___ * _____
_____
_____
_____

0 ___ * _____
_____
_____
_____

0 ___ * _____
_____
_____
_____

JULY

When making friends, it's easier to befriend someone who is already the friend of a friend. Friendship thrives on interconnection.

20 __ * _____
_____
_____
_____

20 __ * _____
_____
_____
_____

20 __ * _____
_____
_____
_____

20 __ * _____
_____
_____
_____

20 __ * _____
_____
_____
_____

JULY

"Great pleasure is to be found not only in keeping
up an old and established friendship but also in
beginning and building up a new one."

—*Seneca*

0 ⬭ * _____

_____

_____

_____

0 ⬭ * _____

_____

_____

_____

0 ⬭ * _____

_____

_____

_____

0 ⬭ * _____

_____

_____

_____

0 ⬭ * _____

_____

_____

_____

6 JULY

A big part of friendship is showing up.

20 __ * _____

_____

_____

_____

20 __ * _____

_____

_____

_____

20 __ * _____

_____

_____

_____

20 __ * _____

_____

_____

_____

20 __ * _____

_____

_____

_____

JULY 7

"A true friend is the greatest of all goods, and of all of them, the one that one least thinks of acquiring."

—*La Rochefoucauld*

0 ⚪ * _____

_____

_____

_____

0 ⚪ * _____

_____

_____

_____

0 ⚪ * _____

_____

_____

_____

0 ⚪ * _____

_____

_____

_____

0 ⚪ * _____

_____

_____

_____

JULY

"Never to wrong others takes one a long way
toward peace of mind."

—*Seneca*

20 __ * _____

_____

_____

_____

20 __ * _____

_____

_____

_____

20 __ * _____

_____

_____

_____

20 __ * _____

_____

_____

_____

20 __ * _____

_____

_____

_____

JULY

In a relationship, it's less important to have many
pleasant experiences than to have fewer unpleasant
experiences; the "negativity bias" means that our
reactions to bad events are faster, stronger, and
stickier than our reactions to good events.

__ * _____

_____

_____

_____

__ * _____

_____

_____

_____

__ * _____

_____

_____

_____

__ * _____

_____

_____

_____

__ * _____

_____

_____

_____

10 JULY

It's easier to prevent pain than to squelch it.
Literally and figuratively.

20 __ * _____

_____

_____

20 __ * _____

_____

_____

20 __ * _____

_____

_____

20 __ * _____

_____

_____

20 __ * _____

_____

_____

JULY

"To know self-restraint and practice it
protects one from shame."

—*Lao Tzu*

0 __ * _____

_____

_____

_____

0 __ * _____

_____

_____

_____

0 __ * _____

_____

_____

_____

0 __ * _____

_____

_____

_____

0 __ * _____

_____

_____

_____

JULY

The most obvious—though perhaps least appealing—
anti-nagging strategy is to do a task yourself.

20 __ * _____
_____
_____
_____

20 __ * _____
_____
_____
_____

20 __ * _____
_____
_____
_____

20 __ * _____
_____
_____
_____

20 __ * _____
_____
_____
_____

JULY

"An uneasy conscience is a hair in the mouth."

—*Mark Twain*

0 __ *_____

_____

_____

_____

0 __ *_____

_____

_____

_____

0 __ *_____

_____

_____

_____

0 __ *_____

_____

_____

_____

0 __ *_____

_____

_____

_____

JULY

Some tasks you should do for *yourself*. When you tell yourself you're doing something for others' benefit, it's easy to expect them to notice and appreciate your work. If you do it for yourself, you won't expect a particular response from others.

20 __ * _____

_____

_____

_____

20 __ * _____

_____

_____

_____

20 __ * _____

_____

_____

_____

20 __ * _____

_____

_____

_____

20 __ * _____

_____

_____

_____

JULY

Tidy areas tend to stay tidy, and messy
areas tend to stay messy.

0 ___ * _____
_____
_____
_____

0 ___ * _____
_____
_____
_____

0 ___ * _____
_____
_____
_____

0 ___ * _____
_____
_____
_____

0 ___ * _____
_____
_____
_____

JULY

People who are rewarded for doing an activity
often stop doing it for fun; being paid turns it into "work."
Let fun stay fun.

20 __ * _____

_____

_____

_____

20 __ * _____

_____

_____

_____

20 __ * _____

_____

_____

_____

20 __ * _____

_____

_____

_____

20 __ * _____

_____

_____

_____

JULY

17

"Children think not of what is past, nor what is to come,
but enjoy the present time, which few of us do."

—Jean de La Bruyère

20 __ * _____

_____

_____

_____

20 __ * _____

_____

_____

_____

20 __ * _____

_____

_____

_____

20 __ * _____

_____

_____

20 __ * _____

_____

_____

_____

JULY

"Enough is abundance to the wise."

—*Euripides*

20 __ * _____

_____

_____

_____

20 __ * _____

_____

_____

_____

20 __ * _____

_____

_____

_____

20 __ * _____

_____

_____

_____

20 __ * _____

_____

_____

_____

JULY

Fun is enjoyable because you don't have to worry about results. You can strive for triumph, or you can putter around, tinker, and explore, without worrying about efficiency or outcomes.

0 __ * _____

_____

_____

_____

0 __ * _____

_____

_____

_____

0 __ * _____

_____

_____

_____

0 __ * _____

_____

_____

_____

0 __ * _____

_____

_____

_____

JULY

Make time for passion. Consider it a real priority instead of an "extra" to be squeezed in when you have some free time. You may never have any free time.

20 __ * _____

_____

_____

_____

20 __ * _____

_____

_____

_____

20 __ * _____

_____

_____

_____

20 __ * _____

_____

_____

_____

20 __ * _____

_____

_____

_____

JULY

21

"There is no duty we so much underrate
as the duty of being happy."

—*Robert Louis Stevenson*

JULY

Some people feel overwhelmed by the question "What's your passion?" It seems large and unanswerable. If so, a useful clue to finding an occupation to pursue, whether for work or play, is to *do* what you *do*.

20 __ * _____

_____

_____

_____

20 __ * _____

_____

_____

_____

20 __ * _____

_____

_____

_____

20 __ * _____

_____

_____

_____

20 __ * _____

_____

_____

_____

JULY

23

"That is happiness; to be dissolved into
something complete and great."

—*Willa Cather*

___ * _____

___ * _____

___ * _____

___ * _____

___ * _____

JULY

Milestone moments are opportunities for evaluation and reflection. Hitting a milestone such as a major birthday, marriage, divorce, a reunion, a death, a birth, or the accomplishment (or not) of a career marker often acts as a catalyst for change.

20 __ * _____

_____

_____

_____

20 __ * _____

_____

_____

_____

20 __ * _____

_____

_____

_____

20 __ * _____

_____

_____

_____

20 __ * _____

_____

_____

_____

JULY

"On the whole, though I never arrived at the perfection I had been so ambitious of obtaining, but fell far short of it, yet as I was, by the endeavor, a better and a happier man than I otherwise should have been had I not attempted it."

—*Benjamin Franklin*

) __ * _____

_____

_____

_____

) __ * _____

_____

_____

_____

) __ * _____

_____

_____

_____

) __ * _____

_____

_____

_____

) __ * _____

_____

_____

_____

JULY

It's easy to make the mistake of thinking that if you have something you love or there's something you want, you'll be happier with more.

20 __ * _____

_____

_____

_____

20 __ * _____

_____

_____

_____

20 __ * _____

_____

_____

_____

20 __ * _____

_____

_____

_____

20 __ * _____

_____

_____

_____

JULY

"Do not spoil what you have by desiring what you have
not; but remember that what you now have was once
among the things only hoped for."

—*Epicurus*

0 __ * _____

_____

_____

_____

0 __ * _____

_____

_____

_____

0 __ * _____

_____

_____

_____

0 __ * _____

_____

_____

_____

0 __ * _____

_____

_____

_____

JULY

"... I do not like having to try to make myself
like things; I like things that make me like them
at once and no trying at all."

—*Samuel Butler*

20 __ * _____

_____

_____

_____

20 __ * _____

_____

_____

_____

20 __ * _____

_____

_____

_____

20 __ * _____

_____

_____

_____

20 __ * _____

_____

_____

_____

JULY

Pursue a passion. Identify it and find time for
it in your ordinary day. Schedule time for it,
like a dentist's appointment.

0 __ * _____

_____

_____

_____

0 __ * _____

_____

_____

_____

0 __ * _____

_____

_____

_____

0 __ * _____

_____

_____

_____

0 __ * _____

_____

_____

_____

JULY

"Nothing can make our life, or the lives of other people,
more beautiful than perpetual kindness."

—*Leo Tolstoy*

20 __ * _____

_____

_____

_____

20 __ * _____

_____

_____

_____

20 __ * _____

_____

_____

_____

20 __ * _____

_____

_____

_____

20 __ * _____

_____

_____

_____

JULY

"There are children who will leave a game to go and be bored in a corner of the garret. How often have I wished or the attic of my boredom when the complications of life made me lose the very germ of all freedom!"

— Gaston Bachelard

0 __ *_____

_____

_____

_____

0 __ *_____

_____

_____

_____

0 __ *_____

_____

_____

_____

_____

0 __ *_____

_____

_____

_____

0 __ *_____

_____

_____

_____

1 AUGUST

Kindness, in everyday life, takes the form of good manner

20 __ * _____

_____

_____

20 __ * _____

_____

_____

20 __ * _____

_____

_____

20 __ * _____

_____

_____

20 __ * _____

_____

_____

AUGUST

"The true spirit of conversation consists more in bringing
out the cleverness of others than in showing a great deal of
it yourself; he who goes away pleased with himself and his
own wit is also greatly pleased with you."

—*Jean de La Bruyère*

0 __ * _____

_____

_____

_____

0 __ * _____

_____

_____

_____

0 __ * _____

_____

_____

_____

0 __ * _____

_____

_____

_____

0 __ * _____

_____

_____

_____

3 AUGUST

Work to be a kinder conversationalist. Look for opportunities to make comments that show your interest in other people's experiences and views.

20 __ * _____
_____
_____
_____

20 __ * _____
_____
_____
_____

20 __ * _____
_____
_____
_____

20 __ * _____
_____
_____
_____

20 __ * _____
_____
_____
_____

AUGUST

"Society and conversation, therefore, are the most powerful remedies for restoring the mind to its tranquillity . . . as well as the best preservatives of that equal and happy temper, which is so necessary to self-satisfaction and enjoyment."

—*Adam Smith*

20 __ * _____

_____

_____

_____

20 __ * _____

_____

_____

_____

20 __ * _____

_____

_____

_____

20 __ * _____

_____

_____

_____

20 __ * _____

_____

_____

_____

AUGUST

5

Forbearance is a form of generosity.

20 __ * _____

_____

_____

20 __ * _____

_____

_____

20 __ * _____

_____

_____

20 __ * _____

_____

_____

20 __ * _____

_____

_____

AUGUST

"Three things in human life are important:
The first is to be kind. The second is to be kind.
And the third is to be kind."

—*Henry James*

) __ * _____

_____

_____

_____

) __ * _____

_____

_____

_____

) __ * _____

_____

_____

_____

) __ * _____

_____

_____

_____

) __ * _____

_____

_____

_____

7 AUGUST

One of the most generous acts is to help someone to *think big*. Words of enthusiasm and confidence from a friend can inspire a person to tackle an ambitious goal.

20 __ * _____
_____
_____
_____

20 __ * _____
_____
_____
_____
_____

20 __ * _____
_____
_____
_____

20 __ * _____
_____
_____
_____

20 __ * _____
_____
_____
_____

AUGUST

how support for a friend who has unhappy news, and also
for a friend who has happy news. It's sometimes more
challenging to be supportive in the face of good fortune.

__ *

__ *

__ *

__ *

__ *

AUGUST

"To treat an enemy with magnanimity
is to blunt our hatred for him."

—*Eric Hoffer*

20 __ * _____
_____
_____
_____

20 __ * _____
_____
_____
_____

20 __ * _____
_____
_____
_____

20 __ * _____
_____
_____
_____

20 __ * _____
_____
_____
_____

AUGUST 10

"We are interested in others when they
are interested in us."

—*Publilius Syrus*

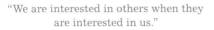 __ * _____

_____

_____

_____

 __ * _____

_____

_____

_____

_____

 __ * _____

_____

_____

_____

 __ * _____

_____

_____

_____

 __ * _____

_____

_____

_____

_____

11 AUGUST

Sometimes it's challenging to give people the laughter they crave, but what starts out as forced laughter can often turn real.

20 ___ * _____

_____

_____

20 ___ * _____

_____

_____

20 ___ * _____

_____

_____

20 ___ * _____

_____

_____

20 ___ * _____

_____

_____

_____

AUGUST

12

"Optimism is true moral courage."

—*Ernest Shakleton*

0 __ * _____

_____

_____

0 __ * _____

_____

_____

0 __ * _____

_____

_____

0 __ * _____

_____

_____

0 __ * _____

_____

_____

13   AUGUST

There's a goofiness to happiness, an innocence, a readiness to be pleased that isn't *cool*. Zest and enthusiasm take energy, humility, and engagement.

20 __ * _____
_____
_____
_____

20 __ * _____
_____
_____
_____

20 __ * _____
_____
_____
_____

20 __ * _____
_____
_____
_____

20 __ * _____
_____
_____
_____

AUGUST

Some people think that happiness isn't a worthy goal;
it's a trivial, American preoccupation, the product of
too much prosperity and too much television. They
think that being happy shows a lack of values, and
that being unhappy is a sign of depth. But being
happy is challenging and estimable.

0 ___ * _____

_____

_____

_____

0 ___ * _____

_____

_____

_____

0 ___ * _____

_____

_____

_____

0 ___ * _____

_____

_____

_____

0 ___ * _____

_____

_____

_____

AUGUST

"How to gain, how to keep, how to recover
happiness is in fact for most men at all times
the secret motive for all they do."

—*William James*

20 __ * _____

_____

_____

_____

20 __ * _____

_____

_____

_____

20 __ * _____

_____

_____

_____

20 __ * _____

_____

_____

_____

20 __ * _____

_____

_____

_____

AUGUST 16

"A small daily task, if it be really daily, will beat the labors of a spasmodic Hercules."

—*Anthony Trollope*

___ * _____
_____
_____
_____

___ * _____
_____
_____
_____

___ * _____
_____
_____
_____

___ * _____
_____
_____
_____

___ * _____
_____
_____
_____

17 AUGUST

If you don't believe you're happy, you're not happy.

20 __ * _____
_____
_____
_____

20 __ * _____
_____
_____
_____

20 __ * _____
_____
_____
_____

20 __ * _____
_____
_____
_____

20 __ * _____
_____
_____
_____

AUGUST

"Many in this world run after felicity like an
absent man hunting for his hat, while all the
time it is on his head or in his hand."

—*Sydney Smith*

20 __ * _____

_____

_____

_____

20 __ * _____

_____

_____

_____

20 __ * _____

_____

_____

_____

20 __ * _____

_____

_____

_____

20 __ * _____

_____

_____

_____

19 AUGUST

Philosophers, scientists, saints, and charlatans all give instruction on how to be happy, but none of this matters to a person who doesn't *want* to be happy.

20 __ *_____

_____

_____

_____

20 __ *_____

_____

_____

_____

20 __ *_____

_____

_____

_____

20 __ *_____

_____

_____

_____

20 __ *_____

_____

_____

_____

AUGUST

"Whatever is worth doing at all is worth doing well."

—Lord Chesterfield

0 __ * _____
_____
_____
_____

0 __ * _____
_____
_____
_____

0 __ * _____
_____
_____
_____

0 __ * _____
_____
_____
_____

0 __ * _____
_____
_____
_____

AUGUST

The satisfaction gained from the achievement of a large undertaking is one of the most substantial that life afford

20 __ * _____

_____

_____

20 __ * _____

_____

_____

20 __ * _____

_____

_____

20 __ * _____

_____

_____

20 __ * _____

_____

_____

AUGUST

22

"The test of a vocation is the love of
the drudgery it involves."

—*Logan Pearsall Smith*

__ * _____

__ * _____

__ * _____

__ * _____

__ * _____

AUGUST

You manage what you measure, so if something is important to you, find a way to measure it. The more abstract the
goal, the more important the measurement.

20 __ * _____

_____

_____

20 __ * _____

_____

_____

20 __ * _____

_____

_____

20 __ * _____

_____

_____

20 __ * _____

_____

_____

AUGUST

Consider the way you think about productive time.
For example, do you work best in lengthy blocks of
uninterrupted time, or in shorter blocks?

0 __ * _____

_____

_____

_____

0 __ * _____

_____

_____

_____

0 __ * _____

_____

_____

_____

0 __ * _____

_____

_____

_____

0 __ * _____

_____

_____

_____

AUGUST

"There can be no joy in living without joy in work."

—*St. Thomas Aquinas*

20 __ * _____

_____

_____

_____

20 __ * _____

_____

_____

_____

20 __ * _____

_____

_____

_____

20 __ * _____

_____

_____

_____

20 __ * _____

_____

_____

_____

AUGUST

"Few lives produce so little happiness as those that are aimless and unoccupied. Apart from all considerations of right and wrong, one of the first conditions of a happy life is that it should be a full and busy one, directed to the attainment of aims outside ourselves."

—*William Edward Hartpole Lecky*

0 __ * _____

_____

_____

_____

0 __ * _____

_____

_____

_____

0 __ * _____

_____

_____

_____

0 __ * _____

_____

_____

_____

0 __ * _____

_____

_____

_____

AUGUST

Unfinished tasks drain energy, and tackling long-delayed tasks is an effective way to boost mood.

20 __ *_____
_____
_____
_____

20 __ *_____
_____
_____
_____

20 __ *_____
_____
_____
_____

20 __ *_____
_____
_____
_____

20 __ *_____
_____
_____
_____

AUGUST

"If we attend continually and promptly to the little that we can do, we shall ere long be surprised to find how little remains that we cannot do."

— *Samuel Butler*

0 ___ * _____

_____

_____

_____

0 ___ * _____

_____

_____

_____

0 ___ * _____

_____

_____

_____

0 ___ * _____

_____

_____

_____

0 ___ * _____

_____

_____

_____

29 AUGUST

Spend out. Don't think about return. Sarah Bernhardt observed, "It is by spending oneself that one becomes rich."

20 __ * _____

_____

_____

_____

20 __ * _____

_____

_____

_____

20 __ * _____

_____

_____

_____

20 __ * _____

_____

_____

_____

20 __ * _____

_____

_____

_____

AUGUST

Pouring out ideas is better for creativity
than doling them out by the teaspoon.

0 ___ * _____
_____
_____
_____

0 ___ * _____
_____
_____
_____

0 ___ * _____
_____
_____
_____

0 ___ * _____
_____
_____
_____

0 ___ * _____
_____
_____
_____

AUGUST

"Best is good. Better is best."

—*Lisa Grunwald*

20 __ * _____

_____

_____

_____

20 __ * _____

_____

_____

_____

20 __ * _____

_____

_____

_____

20 __ * _____

_____

_____

_____

20 __ * _____

_____

_____

_____

SEPTEMBER

1

Give something up. Sometimes it feels good to say,
"I'm going to stop!" "No more!" or "That's the last time."

0 ⬯ * _____
_____
_____
_____

0 ⬯ * _____
_____
_____
_____

0 ⬯ * _____
_____
_____
_____

0 ⬯ * _____
_____
_____
_____

0 ⬯ * _____
_____
_____
_____

SEPTEMBER

"You increase your self-respect when you feel you've done everything you ought to have done, and if there is nothing else to enjoy, there remains that chief of pleasures, the feeling of being pleased with oneself."

—*Eugène Delacroix*

20 __ * _____

_____

_____

_____

20 __ * _____

_____

_____

_____

20 __ * _____

_____

_____

_____

20 __ * _____

_____

_____

_____

20 __ * _____

_____

_____

_____

SEPTEMBER

Don't force yourself to try to like things.
Spend some time on things that you already like.

0 __ * _____

_____

_____

_____

0 __ * _____

_____

_____

_____

0 __ * _____

_____

_____

_____

0 __ * _____

_____

_____

_____

0 __ * _____

_____

_____

_____

SEPTEMBER

"One of the best and fastest ways of acquiring knowledge is to insist on remaining ignorant about things that aren't worth knowing."

—*Sydney Harris*

20 __ *_____

_____

_____

_____

20 __ *_____

_____

_____

_____

20 __ *_____

_____

_____

_____

20 __ *_____

_____

_____

_____

20 __ *_____

_____

_____

_____

SEPTEMBER

For it is always wiser to consider not so much why a thing
is not enjoyable, as why we ourselves do not enjoy it."

—G. K. Chesterton

0 ___ * _____

_____

_____

0 ___ * _____

_____

_____

0 ___ * _____

_____

_____

0 ___ * _____

_____

_____

0 ___ * _____

_____

_____

SEPTEMBER

If you don't know what to do for fun, ask yourself,
"What did I enjoy doing when I was ten years old?"
An activity you enjoyed as a ten-year-old is probably
something you'd enjoy now.

20 __ * _____

_____

_____

_____

20 __ * _____

_____

_____

_____

20 __ * _____

_____

_____

_____

20 __ * _____

_____

_____

_____

20 __ * _____

_____

_____

_____

SEPTEMBER

7

Embrace a collection. A collection provides a mission, a reason to visit new places, the excitement of the chase, a field of expertise (no matter how trivial), and, often, a bond with other people.

) ⬭ * _____

) ⬭ * _____

) ⬭ * _____

) ⬭ * _____

) ⬭ * _____

SEPTEMBER

"Indolence is a delightful but distressing state:
We must be doing something to be happy."

—*William Hazlitt*

20 __ * _____

_____

_____

_____

20 __ * _____

_____

_____

_____

20 __ * _____

_____

_____

_____

20 __ * _____

_____

_____

_____

20 __ * _____

_____

_____

_____

SEPTEMBER

"In order that people may be happy in their work,
these three things are needed: They must be fit for it.
They must not do too much of it. And they must have
a sense of success in it."

—*John Ruskin*

) ___ * _____

_____

_____

_____

) ___ * _____

_____

_____

_____

) ___ * _____

_____

_____

_____

) ___ * _____

_____

_____

_____

) ___ * _____

_____

_____

_____

10 SEPTEMBER

"The supreme accomplishment is to blur
the line between work and play."

—*Arnold Toynbee*

20 __ * _____

_____

_____

_____

20 __ * _____

_____

_____

_____

20 __ * _____

_____

_____

_____

20 __ * _____

_____

_____

_____

20 __ * _____

_____

_____

_____

SEPTEMBER

11

Happiness is a critical factor for work, and work is a critical factor for happiness. In one of those life-isn't-fair results, the happy outperform the less happy.

__ *_____

_____

_____

_____

__ *_____

_____

_____

_____

__ *_____

_____

_____

_____

__ *_____

_____

_____

_____

__ *_____

_____

_____

_____

12 SEPTEMBER

"A man does not work only for the sake of producing, but
to set a value on his time. We feel more satisfied with our
selves and with our day if we have stirred up our minds
and made a good start, or have finished a piece of work."

—*Eugène Delacroix*

20 __ * _____
_____
_____
_____

20 __ * _____
_____
_____
_____

20 __ * _____
_____
_____
_____

20 __ * _____
_____
_____
_____

20 __ * _____
_____
_____
_____

SEPTEMBER

Novelty is stimulating and valuable. However, the pleasure of doing a thing in the same way, at the same time, every day, and savoring it, is worth noting.

20 __ * _____

_____

_____

_____

20 __ * _____

_____

_____

_____

20 __ * _____

_____

_____

_____

20 __ * _____

_____

_____

_____

20 __ * _____

_____

_____

_____

14 SEPTEMBER

"Actually, I jade very quickly. Once is usually enough.
Either once only, or every day. If you do something
once it's exciting, and if you do it every day it's exciting.
But if you do it, say, twice or just almost every day,
it's not good anymore."

—*Andy Warhol*

20 __ * _____

_____

_____

_____

20 __ * _____

_____

_____

_____

20 __ * _____

_____

_____

_____

20 __ * _____

_____

_____

_____

20 __ * _____

_____

_____

_____

SEPTEMBER

One of the best ways to make *yourself* happy is to make *other people* happy. One of the best ways to make *other people* happy is to be happy *yourself*.

20 __ * _____

_____

_____

_____

20 __ * _____

_____

_____

_____

20 __ * _____

_____

_____

_____

20 __ * _____

_____

_____

_____

20 __ * _____

_____

_____

_____

16 SEPTEMBER

"Imaginary evil is romantic and varied; real evil is gloomy, monotonous, barren, boring. Imaginary good is boring; real good is always new, marvelous, intoxicating."

— Simone Weil

20 __ * _____

_____

_____

_____

20 __ * _____

_____

_____

_____

20 __ * _____

_____

_____

_____

20 __ * _____

_____

_____

_____

20 __ * _____

_____

_____

_____

SEPTEMBER 17

There is an "I" in "happiness."

0 ___ * _____

_____

_____

0 ___ * _____

_____

_____

0 ___ * _____

_____

_____

0 ___ * _____

_____

_____

0 ___ * _____

_____

_____

18 SEPTEMBER

"To be really happy and really safe, one ought to have at least two or three hobbies, and they must all be real."

—*Winston Churchill*

20 __ * _____
_____
_____
_____

20 __ * _____
_____
_____
_____

20 __ * _____
_____
_____
_____

20 __ * _____
_____
_____
_____

20 __ * _____
_____
_____
_____

SEPTEMBER

There are three categories of fun: challenging fun, the most demanding and most rewarding type of fun; accommodating fun, which also takes effort; and relaxing fun, which requires no skill or action.

'0 ___ * _____

_____

_____

_____

'0 ___ * _____

_____

_____

_____

'0 ___ * _____

_____

_____

_____

'0 ___ * _____

_____

_____

_____

0 ___ * _____

_____

_____

_____

20 SEPTEMBER

"Happiness does not reside in strength or money;
it lies in rightness and many-sidedness."

—Democritus

20 __ * _____
_____
_____
_____

20 __ * _____
_____
_____
_____

20 __ * _____
_____
_____
_____

20 __ * _____
_____
_____
_____

20 __ * _____
_____
_____
_____

SEPTEMBER

Don't always worry about being efficient.
Exploration, experimentation, and digression
don't necessarily *look* productive.

) __ *_____
_____
_____
_____

) __ *_____
_____
_____
_____

) __ *_____
_____
_____
_____

) __ *_____
_____
_____
_____

) __ *_____
_____
_____
_____

SEPTEMBER

"All knowledge is interesting to a wise man."

—*Matthew Arnold*

20 __ * _____

_____

_____

_____

20 __ * _____

_____

_____

_____

20 __ * _____

_____

_____

_____

20 __ * _____

_____

_____

_____

20 __ * _____

_____

_____

_____

SEPTEMBER

Go off the path: Find ways to encounter the unexpected thoughts, unfamiliar scenes, new people, and unconventional juxtapositions that are key sources of creative energy and happiness.

__ * _____

__ * _____

__ * _____

__ * _____

__ * _____

24 SEPTEMBER

"Curiosity is one of the permanent and certain characteristics of a vigorous intellect. Every advance into knowledge opens new prospects and produces new incitements to farther progress."

—Samuel Johnson

20 __ * _____

_____

_____

_____

20 __ * _____

_____

_____

_____

20 __ * _____

_____

_____

_____

20 __ * _____

_____

_____

_____

20 __ * _____

_____

_____

_____

SEPTEMBER

"The satisfaction to be derived from success in
a great constructive enterprise is one of the
most massive that life has to offer."

—*Bertrand Russell*

0 __ *_____

_____

_____

0 __ *_____

_____

_____

0 __ *_____

_____

_____

0 __ *_____

_____

_____

0 __ *_____

_____

_____

SEPTEMBER

Devising some physical way of preserving
information—such as an idea board, scrapbook,
or commonplace book—keeps good ideas vivid
and creates unexpected juxtapositions.

20 __ * _____
_____
_____

20 __ * _____
_____
_____

20 __ * _____
_____
_____

20 __ * _____
_____
_____

20 __ * _____
_____
_____

SEPTEMBER

"Things won are done; joy's soul lies in doing."

—*William Shakespeare*

 * _____
_____
_____
_____

* _____
_____
_____
_____

* _____
_____
_____
_____

* _____
_____
_____
_____

* _____
_____
_____
_____

28 SEPTEMBER

If you're willing to accept blame when you deserve it,
people will be more willing to trust you with responsibilit

20 __ * _____

_____

_____

20 __ * _____

_____

_____

20 __ * _____

_____

_____

20 __ * _____

_____

_____

20 __ * _____

_____

_____

SEPTEMBER

Spending time with children allows us to experience our own sincere enjoyment of activities—going to the circus, decorating cookies, making balloon animals—that we wouldn't undertake on our own.

20 __ *_____
_____
_____

20 __ *_____
_____
_____

20 __ *_____
_____
_____

20 __ *_____
_____
_____

20 __ *_____
_____
_____
_____

30 SEPTEMBER

"The deepest principle in human nature is
the craving to be appreciated."

—William James

20 __ * _____
_____
_____
_____

20 __ * _____
_____
_____
_____

20 __ * _____
_____
_____
_____

20 __ * _____
_____
_____
_____

20 __ * _____
_____
_____
_____

OCTOBER

1

Consider how a question might strike another person. You may think you're showing a polite interest, but some questions—"Have you found a job yet?" "When are you going to start a family?"—might rub someone the wrong way. Show an interest with more open-ended questions, like "What are you up to these days?" or "What's keeping you busy?"

20 __ * _____

_____

_____

_____

20 __ * _____

_____

_____

_____

20 __ * _____

_____

_____

_____

20 __ * _____

_____

_____

20 __ * _____

_____

_____

_____

OCTOBER

"One can have no smaller or greater mastery
than mastery of oneself."

—*Leonardo da Vinci*

20 __ * _____

_____

_____

_____

20 __ * _____

_____

_____

_____

20 __ * _____

_____

_____

_____

20 __ * _____

_____

_____

_____

20 __ * _____

_____

_____

_____

OCTOBER

"The happiness of those who want to be popular depends on others; the happiness of those who seek pleasure fluctuates with moods outside their control; but the happiness of the wise grows out of their own free acts."

—*Marcus Aurelius*

0 __ * _____

_____

_____

_____

0 __ * _____

_____

_____

_____

0 __ * _____

_____

_____

_____

0 __ * _____

_____

_____

_____

0 __ * _____

_____

_____

_____

4 OCTOBER

To help yourself stick to your resolutions, review them each day and find a way to hold yourself accountable.

20 __ * _____

_____

_____

20 __ * _____

_____

_____

20 __ * _____

_____

_____

20 __ * _____

_____

_____

20 __ * _____

_____

_____

OCTOBER

"If you look at a thing, the very fact of your looking changes it . . . if you think about yourself, that very fact changes you."

—*Robert Penn Warren*

20 __ * _____

_____

_____

_____

20 __ * _____

_____

_____

_____

20 __ * _____

_____

_____

_____

20 __ * _____

_____

_____

_____

20 __ * _____

_____

_____

_____

6 OCTOBER

Happy people make people happy.
But you can't *make* someone be happy.

20 ___ * _____
_____
_____
_____

20 ___ * _____
_____
_____
_____

20 ___ * _____
_____
_____
_____

20 ___ * _____
_____
_____
_____

20 ___ * _____
_____
_____
_____

OCTOBER

7

To keep loneliness at bay, you need at least one close relationship with someone in whom you can confide (not just a pal with whom you talk about impersonal subjects).

0 ___ * _____

_____

_____

_____

0 ___ * _____

_____

_____

_____

0 ___ * _____

_____

_____

_____

0 ___ * _____

_____

_____

_____

0 ___ * _____

_____

_____

_____

OCTOBER

"We are so accustomed to disguising our true nature from others, that we end up disguising it from ourselves."

—*La Rochefoucauld*

20 __ * _____

_____

_____

20 __ * _____

_____

_____

_____

20 __ * _____

_____

_____

_____

20 __ * _____

_____

_____

_____

20 __ * _____

_____

_____

_____

OCTOBER

We all need intimate relationships, to be able to confide in others, to belong. Aim to build a relationship network in which you can both give and receive support.

0 __ * _____

_____

_____

_____

0 __ * _____

_____

_____

_____

0 __ * _____

_____

_____

_____

0 __ * _____

_____

_____

_____

0 __ * _____

_____

_____

_____

10 OCTOBER

"He who is and remains true to himself and to others has the most attractive quality of the greatest talents."

—*Goethe*

20 ___ * _____

_____

_____

_____

20 ___ * _____

_____

_____

_____

20 ___ * _____

_____

_____

_____

20 ___ * _____

_____

_____

_____

20 ___ * _____

_____

_____

_____

OCTOBER

11

"It is essential to happiness that our way of living should spring from our own deep impulses and not from the accidental tastes and desires of those who happen to be our neighbors, or even our relations."

—*Bertrand Russell*

20 __ * _____

_____

_____

_____

20 __ * _____

_____

_____

_____

20 __ * _____

_____

_____

_____

20 __ * _____

_____

_____

_____

20 __ * _____

_____

_____

_____

OCTOBER

It doesn't matter what you wish you were like.
You are who you are.

20 ___ * _____
_____
_____
_____

20 ___ * _____
_____
_____
_____

20 ___ * _____
_____
_____
_____

20 ___ * _____
_____
_____
_____

20 ___ * _____
_____
_____
_____

OCTOBER

Beware of false choices. For example, sometimes people assume that they have to choose between lots of superficial friends and a few intimate friends. But that's a false choice.

0 __ * _____

_____

_____

_____

0 __ * _____

_____

_____

_____

0 __ * _____

_____

_____

_____

0 __ * _____

_____

_____

_____

0 __ * _____

_____

_____

_____

14 OCTOBER

"The greatest achievement of the human spirit is
to live up to one's opportunities and make the most
of one's resources."

—Marquis de Vauvenargues

20 __ *_____

_____

_____

_____

20 __ *_____

_____

_____

_____

20 __ *_____

_____

_____

_____

20 __ *_____

_____

_____

_____

20 __ *_____

_____

_____

_____

OCTOBER

"The best way to cheer yourself is to try
to cheer somebody else up."

—*Mark Twain*

20 __ * _____

_____

_____

_____

20 __ * _____

_____

_____

_____

20 __ * _____

_____

_____

_____

20 __ * _____

_____

_____

_____

20 __ * _____

_____

_____

_____

16 OCTOBER

People who enjoy silliness are more likely to feel happy.

20 __ * _____
_____
_____
_____

20 __ * _____
_____
_____
_____

20 __ * _____
_____
_____
_____

20 __ * _____
_____
_____
_____

20 __ * _____
_____
_____
_____

OCTOBER

Although people prefer different social situations, extroverts and introverts alike get a boost from connecting with others.

0 ⬚ * _____

_____

_____

_____

0 ⬚ * _____

_____

_____

_____

0 ⬚ * _____

_____

_____

_____

0 ⬚ * _____

_____

_____

_____

0 ⬚ * _____

_____

_____

_____

OCTOBER

"Everything that irritates us about others can lead us to an understanding of ourselves."

—Carl Jung

20 __ * _____

_____

_____

_____

20 __ * _____

_____

_____

_____

20 __ * _____

_____

_____

_____

20 __ * _____

_____

_____

_____

20 __ * _____

_____

_____

_____

OCTOBER

"They always say that time changes things, but actually
you have to change them yourself."

—Andy Warhol

0 __ * _____

_____

_____

_____

0 __ * _____

_____

_____

_____

0 __ * _____

_____

_____

_____

0 __ * _____

_____

_____

_____

0 __ * _____

_____

_____

_____

20 OCTOBER

Appreciate your body. For example, instead of worrying about your weight, think about all the activities that your body permits.

20 __ * _____

_____

_____

_____

20 __ * _____

_____

_____

_____

20 __ * _____

_____

_____

_____

20 __ * _____

_____

_____

_____

20 __ * _____

_____

_____

_____

OCTOBER

"It is one of the saddest facts of human nature that we commonly only learn their value [of blessings] by their loss. . . . There are times in the lives of most of us when we would have given all the world to be as we were but yesterday, though that yesterday had passed over us unappreciated and unenjoyed."

—William Edward Hartpole Lecky

20 __ * _____

_____

_____

_____

20 __ * _____

_____

_____

_____

20 __ * _____

_____

_____

_____

20 __ * _____

_____

_____

_____

20 __ * _____

_____

_____

_____

OCTOBER

Find a mental "area of refuge." Find thoughts and memories that make you happy and turn to them when you find yourself dwelling on bad feelings.

20 __ * _____

_____

_____

_____

20 __ * _____

_____

_____

_____

20 __ * _____

_____

_____

_____

20 __ * _____

_____

_____

_____

20 __ * _____

_____

_____

_____

OCTOBER 23

"Bees, by the instinct of nature, do love their hives,
and birds their nests."

—John Bramhall

20 __ * _____

_____

_____

_____

20 __ * _____

_____

_____

_____

20 __ * _____

_____

_____

_____

20 __ * _____

_____

_____

_____

20 __ * _____

_____

_____

_____

OCTOBER

We expect heroic virtue to look flashy, but ordinary life is full of opportunities for worthy, if inconspicuous, virtue.

20 __ * _____
_____
_____
_____

20 __ * _____
_____
_____
_____

20 __ * _____
_____
_____
_____

20 __ * _____
_____
_____
_____

20 __ * _____
_____
_____
_____

OCTOBER

> "Human Felicity is produced not so much by great
> Pieces of good Fortune that seldom happen, as by
> little Advantages that occur every Day."

—Benjamin Franklin

0 __ * _____

_____

_____

_____

0 __ * _____

_____

_____

_____

0 __ * _____

_____

_____

_____

0 __ * _____

_____

_____

_____

0 __ * _____

_____

_____

_____

OCTOBER

"To give up pretensions is as blessed
a relief as to get them gratified."

—*William James*

20 __ * _____

_____

_____

_____

20 __ * _____

_____

_____

_____

20 __ * _____

_____

_____

_____

20 __ * _____

_____

_____

_____

20 __ * _____

_____

_____

_____

OCTOBER

People's basic psychological needs include the need to feel secure, to feel good at what they do, to be loved, to feel connected to others, and to have a strong sense of control.

20 __ * _____

_____

_____

_____

20 __ * _____

_____

_____

_____

20 __ * _____

_____

_____

_____

20 __ * _____

_____

_____

_____

20 __ * _____

_____

_____

_____

28 OCTOBER

"Self-reverence, self-knowledge, self-control.
These three alone lead life to sovereign power."

—*Alfred Lord Tennyson*

20 __ * _____

_____

_____

20 __ * _____

_____

_____

20 __ * _____

_____

_____

20 __ * _____

_____

_____

20 __ * _____

_____

_____

OCTOBER

Money is a good servant but a bad master.
To enhance happiness, spend money to support
aspects of life that themselves bring happiness.

20 __ * _____

_____

_____

_____

20 __ * _____

_____

_____

_____

20 __ * _____

_____

_____

_____

20 __ * _____

_____

_____

_____

20 __ * _____

_____

_____

_____

30 OCTOBER

"It is in no man's power to have whatever he wants; but he has it in his power not to wish for what he hasn't got, and cheerfully make the most of the things that do come his way."

—*Seneca*

20 __ * _____

_____

_____

20 __ * _____

_____

_____

20 __ * _____

_____

_____

20 __ * _____

_____

_____

20 __ * _____

_____

_____

OCTOBER

"We seldom think of what we have but
always of what we lack."

—*Schopenhauer*

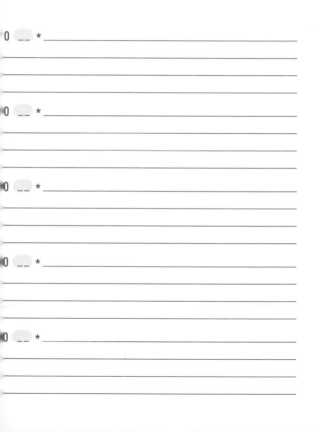

1 NOVEMBER

One of the best ways to make yourself happy in the *present* is to reflect on happy times from the *past*.

20 __ * _____

_____

_____

20 __ * _____

_____

_____

20 __ * _____

_____

_____

20 __ * _____

_____

_____

20 __ * _____

_____

_____

_____

NOVEMBER

"Good humor may be defined as a habit of being pleased; a constant and perennial softness of manner, easiness of approach, and suavity of disposition."

— *Samuel Johnson*

0 __ * _____

_____

_____

_____

0 __ * _____

_____

_____

_____

0 __ * _____

_____

_____

_____

0 __ * _____

_____

_____

_____

0 __ * _____

_____

_____

_____

NOVEMBER

Look for ways to record the fleeting moments that make life sweet but that so easily vanish from memory. Expressing and recalling your feelings will amplify the effect of happy experiences.

20 __ * _____

_____

_____

_____

20 __ * _____

_____

_____

_____

20 __ * _____

_____

_____

_____

20 __ * _____

_____

_____

_____

20 __ * _____

_____

_____

_____

NOVEMBER

"When you are content to be simply yourself and don't
compare or compete, everybody will respect you."

—Lao Tzu

20 __ * _____

_____

_____

_____

20 __ * _____

_____

_____

_____

20 __ * _____

_____

_____

_____

20 __ * _____

_____

_____

_____

20 __ * _____

_____

_____

_____

5 NOVEMBER

"Everything is raw material. Everything is relevant.
Everything is usable. Everything feeds into my
creativity. But without proper preparation,
I cannot see it, retain it, and use it."

— Twyla Tharp

20 ___ * _____

_____

_____

_____

20 ___ * _____

_____

_____

_____

20 ___ * _____

_____

_____

_____

20 ___ * _____

_____

_____

_____

20 ___ * _____

_____

_____

_____

NOVEMBER

One of the great paradoxes of happiness is that we seek to control our lives, but the unfamiliar and the unexpected are important sources of happiness.

0 __ * _____

0 __ * _____

0 __ * _____

0 __ * _____

0 __ * _____

NOVEMBER

"To a great experience one thing is essential,
an experiencing nature. It is not enough to have
opportunity, it is essential to feel it."

—Walter Bagehot

20 __ * _____

_____

_____

_____

20 __ * _____

_____

_____

_____

20 __ * _____

_____

_____

_____

20 __ * _____

_____

_____

_____

20 __ * _____

_____

_____

_____

NOVEMBER

"If you would be loved, love and be lovable."

—*Benjamin Franklin*

20 __ * _____

_____

_____

_____

20 __ * _____

_____

_____

_____

20 __ * _____

_____

_____

_____

20 __ * _____

_____

_____

_____

20 __ * _____

_____

_____

_____

NOVEMBER

Build a treasure house of happy memories. Find ways to memorialize little family jokes and funny incidents, birthday parties, and holiday dinners.

20 __ * _____

_____

_____

_____

20 __ * _____

_____

_____

_____

20 __ * _____

_____

_____

_____

20 __ * _____

_____

_____

_____

20 __ * _____

_____

_____

_____

NOVEMBER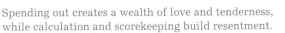

Spending out creates a wealth of love and tenderness,
while calculation and scorekeeping build resentment.

20 __ * _____
_____
_____
_____

20 __ * _____
_____
_____
_____

20 __ * _____
_____
_____
_____

20 __ * _____
_____
_____
_____

20 __ * _____
_____
_____
_____

11 NOVEMBER

"The true secret of happiness *lies in the taking a genuine interest in all the details of daily life*."

—*William Morris*

20 __ * _____
_____
_____
_____

20 __ * _____
_____
_____
_____

20 __ * _____
_____
_____
_____

20 __ * _____
_____
_____
_____

20 __ * _____
_____
_____
_____

NOVEMBER 12

Familiarity breeds affection. The "mere exposure effect" describes the fact that repeated exposure makes people like faces, music, even nonsense syllables, better.

20 __ * _____

_____

_____

_____

20 __ * _____

_____

_____

_____

20 __ * _____

_____

_____

_____

20 __ * _____

_____

_____

20 __ * _____

_____

_____

_____

NOVEMBER

"If you add a little to a little and do this often,
soon the little will become great."

—*Hesiod*

20 __ * _____
_____
_____
_____

20 __ * _____
_____
_____
_____

20 __ * _____
_____
_____
_____

20 __ * _____
_____
_____
_____

20 __ * _____
_____
_____
_____

NOVEMBER 14

"Seek to learn constantly while you live; do not wait in the faith that old age by itself will bring wisdom."

—*Solon*

20 __ * _____

_____

_____

20 __ * _____

_____

_____

20 __ * _____

_____

_____

20 __ * _____

_____

_____

20 __ * _____

_____

_____

_____

15 NOVEMBER

What makes you happy is to spend money on things *you* value—and it takes self-knowledge and discipline to discover what *you* really want.

20 __ * _____

_____

_____

20 __ * _____

_____

_____

20 __ * _____

_____

_____

20 __ * _____

_____

_____

20 __ * _____

_____

_____

_____

NOVEMBER

Because money permits a constant stream of luxuries
and indulgences, it can take away their savor; by
permitting instant gratification, it shortcuts the
happiness of anticipation.

20 __ * _____

_____

_____

_____

20 __ * _____

_____

_____

_____

20 __ * _____

_____

_____

_____

20 __ * _____

_____

_____

_____

20 __ * _____

_____

_____

_____

NOVEMBER

"The conduct of our lives is the true
reflection of our thoughts."

—*Michel de Montaigne*

20 __ * _____

_____

_____

_____

20 __ * _____

_____

_____

_____

20 __ * _____

_____

_____

_____

20 __ * _____

_____

_____

_____

20 __ * _____

_____

_____

_____

NOVEMBER

"True contentment is a thing as active as agriculture.
It is the power of getting out of any situation all that
there is in it. It is arduous and it is rare."

—*G. K. Chesterton*

20 __ * _____

_____

_____

20 __ * _____

_____

_____

20 __ * _____

_____

_____

20 __ * _____

_____

_____

20 __ * _____

_____

_____

_____

19 NOVEMBER

Scrimping, saving, imagining, planning, hoping—
these stages enlarge the happiness we feel.

20 __ * _____

_____

_____

_____

20 __ * _____

_____

_____

_____

20 __ * _____

_____

_____

_____

20 __ * _____

_____

_____

_____

20 __ * _____

_____

_____

_____

NOVEMBER

"When one has money one feels no joy in possessing it, but when money is lacking one misses the enjoyments it provides."

— *Eugène Delacroix*

20 __ * _____

_____

_____

20 __ * _____

_____

_____

20 __ * _____

_____

_____

20 __ * _____

_____

_____

20 __ * _____

_____

_____

21 NOVEMBER

Enthusiasm is a form of social courage.

20 __ * _____

_____

_____

20 __ * _____

_____

_____

20 __ * _____

_____

_____

20 __ * _____

_____

_____

20 __ * _____

_____

_____

_____

NOVEMBER

"We act as though comfort and luxury were the
chief requirements of life, when all we need to make us
happy is something to be enthusiastic about."

—*Charles Kingsley*

20 __ * _____

20 __ * _____

20 __ * _____

20 __ * _____

20 __ * _____

NOVEMBER

"Home, I learned, can be anywhere you make it. Home is also the place to which you come back again and again."

—*Margaret Mead*

20 __ * _____

_____

_____

_____

20 __ * _____

_____

_____

_____

20 __ * _____

_____

_____

_____

20 __ * _____

_____

_____

_____

20 __ * _____

_____

_____

_____

NOVEMBER

In the long run, traditions help sustain family bonds, but
not everyone is interested in keeping up traditions.
If tradition isn't important to you, nevertheless try to play
your part patiently. If tradition is important to you, try to
relax and enjoy the day, whatever happens.

20 __ * _____

_____

_____

20 __ * _____

_____

_____

20 __ * _____

_____

_____

20 __ * _____

_____

_____

20 __ * _____

_____

_____

25 NOVEMBER

"A comfortable home is a great source of happiness.
It ranks immediately after health and a good conscience."

—Sydney Smith

20 __ * _____

_____

_____

_____

20 __ * _____

_____

_____

_____

20 __ * _____

_____

_____

_____

20 __ * _____

_____

_____

_____

20 __ * _____

_____

_____

_____

NOVEMBER 26

"Three grand essentials to happiness in this life are something to do, something to love, and something to hope for."

—*Joseph Addison*

20 __ * _____

_____

_____

20 __ * _____

_____

_____

20 __ * _____

_____

_____

20 __ * _____

_____

_____

20 __ * _____

_____

_____

NOVEMBER

Enthusiasm requires humility. A willingness to be pleased requires modesty and even innocence.

20 __ * _____

_____

_____

20 __ * _____

_____

_____

20 __ * _____

_____

_____

20 __ * _____

_____

_____

20 __ * _____

_____

_____

_____

NOVEMBER

"The habit of being happy enables one to be freed, or largely freed, from the dominance of outward conditions."

—Robert Louis Stevenson

20 __ * _____

_____

_____

_____

20 __ * _____

_____

_____

_____

20 __ * _____

_____

_____

_____

20 __ * _____

_____

_____

_____

20 __ * _____

_____

_____

_____

NOVEMBER

"Iron rusts from disuse, stagnant water loses its purity,
and in cold weather becomes frozen; even so does inaction
sap the vigor of the mind."

—*Leonardo da Vinci*

20 __ * _____

_____

_____

_____

20 __ * _____

_____

_____

_____

20 __ * _____

_____

_____

_____

20 __ * _____

_____

_____

_____

20 __ * _____

_____

_____

_____

NOVEMBER

"Anything one does every day is important and imposing
and anywhere one lives is interesting and beautiful."

—*Gertrude Stein*

20 __ * _____

_____

_____

20 __ * _____

_____

_____

20 __ * _____

_____

_____

20 __ * _____

_____

_____

20 __ * _____

_____

_____

1 DECEMBER

Family traditions make occasions feel special and exciting.
They mark the passage of time in a happy way, and they
provide a sense of anticipation, security, and continuity.

20 __ * _____
_____
_____
_____

20 __ * _____
_____
_____
_____

20 __ * _____
_____
_____
_____

20 __ * _____
_____
_____
_____

20 __ * _____
_____
_____
_____

DECEMBER

"An aim is the only fortune worth finding; and it is not to be found in foreign lands but in the heart itself."

—*Robert Louis Stevenson*

20 __ * _____

_____

_____

20 __ * _____

_____

_____

20 __ * _____

_____

_____

20 __ * _____

_____

_____

20 __ * _____

_____

_____

DECEMBER

Play is not merely idle time; it's an opportunity
to experiment with new interests and to draw
closer to other people.

20 ___ * _____
_____
_____
_____

20 ___ * _____
_____
_____
_____

20 ___ * _____
_____
_____
_____

20 ___ * _____
_____
_____
_____

20 ___ * _____
_____
_____
_____

DECEMBER 4

"Find expression for a joy, and you intensify its ecstasy."

—*Oscar Wilde*

20 __ *_____
_____
_____
_____

20 __ *_____
_____
_____
_____

20 __ *_____
_____
_____
_____

20 __ *_____
_____
_____
_____

20 __ *_____
_____
_____
_____

DECEMBER

To eke out the most happiness from an experience,
anticipate it, *savor* it as it unfolds, *express* happiness,
and *recall* a happy memory.

20 __ * _____
_____
_____
_____

20 __ * _____
_____
_____
_____

20 __ * _____
_____
_____
_____

20 __ * _____
_____
_____
_____

20 __ * _____
_____
_____
_____

DECEMBER

"The passing moment is all we can be sure of; it is only common sense to extract its utmost value from it; the future will one day be the present and will seem as unimportant as the present does now."

—*W. Somerset Maugham*

20 __ * _____

_____

_____

_____

20 __ * _____

_____

_____

_____

20 __ * _____

_____

_____

_____

20 __ * _____

_____

_____

_____

20 __ * _____

_____

_____

_____

7 DECEMBER

Find time for fun. Always choosing to work instead of play can make you feel more virtuous but also more drained.

20 __ * _____

_____

_____

_____

20 __ * _____

_____

_____

_____

20 __ * _____

_____

_____

_____

20 __ * _____

_____

_____

_____

20 __ * _____

_____

_____

_____

DECEMBER

"Now of all those qualities the one that most immediately
makes us happy is cheerfulness of disposition; for this
good quality is its own instantaneous reward."

—*Schopenhauer*

20 __ * _____

_____

_____

_____

20 __ * _____

_____

_____

_____

20 __ * _____

_____

_____

_____

20 __ * _____

_____

_____

_____

20 __ * _____

_____

_____

_____

DECEMBER

There's no need to wait for traditions to emerge spontaneously. A "new tradition" may be an oxymoron, but that shouldn't prevent the invention of a tradition you wish you had.

20 __ * _____

_____

_____

_____

20 __ * _____

_____

_____

_____

20 __ * _____

_____

_____

_____

20 __ * _____

_____

_____

_____

20 __ * _____

_____

_____

_____

DECEMBER

10

"The time you enjoy wasting is not wasted time."

—*Bertrand Russell*

20 __ * _____

_____

_____

_____

20 __ * _____

_____

_____

_____

20 __ * _____

_____

_____

_____

20 __ * _____

_____

_____

_____

20 __ * _____

_____

_____

_____

11 | DECEMBER

"When you meet someone better than yourself,
turn your thoughts to becoming his equal."

—*Confucius*

20 __ * _____

_____

_____

_____

20 __ * _____

_____

_____

_____

20 __ * _____

_____

_____

_____

20 __ * _____

_____

_____

_____

20 __ * _____

_____

_____

_____

DECEMBER

"The politeness of mind consists in thinking
of honest and delicate things."

—*La Rochefoucauld*

20 __ *_____

_____

_____

_____

20 __ *_____

_____

_____

_____

20 __ *_____

_____

_____

_____

20 __ *_____

_____

_____

_____

20 __ *_____

_____

_____

_____

13 DECEMBER

Take photographs. Pictures will help you recall happy details that now seem unforgettable.

20 __ *_____
_____
_____
_____

20 __ *_____
_____
_____
_____

20 __ *_____
_____
_____
_____

20 __ *_____
_____
_____
_____

20 __ *_____
_____
_____
_____

DECEMBER

"You can observe a lot by watching."

— *Yogi Berra*

20 __ * _____

_____

_____

_____

20 __ * _____

_____

_____

20 __ * _____

_____

_____

20 __ * _____

_____

_____

20 __ * _____

_____

_____

_____

15 DECEMBER

Look for ways to keep happy memories vivid. Recalling happy times helps boost happiness in the present.

20 __ * _____
_____
_____
_____

20 __ * _____
_____
_____
_____

20 __ * _____
_____
_____
_____

20 __ * _____
_____
_____
_____

20 __ * _____
_____
_____
_____

DECEMBER

16

"Felicity is in taste and not in things; and it is by having what one loves that one is happy, and not by having what others find agreeable."

— *La Rochefoucauld*

20 __ * _____
_____
_____
_____

20 __ * _____
_____
_____
_____

20 __ * _____
_____
_____
_____

20 __ * _____
_____
_____
_____

20 __ * _____
_____
_____
_____

17 DECEMBER

Technology is a good servant but a bad master.
Look for ways to make sure technology is playing its
proper role in your life.

20 __ * _____
_____
_____
_____

20 __ * _____
_____
_____
_____

20 __ * _____
_____
_____
_____

20 __ * _____
_____
_____
_____

20 __ * _____
_____
_____
_____

DECEMBER

"There are no new truths, but only truths that have not been recognized by those who have perceived them without noticing."

—Mary McCarthy

20 __ * _____

_____

_____

_____

20 __ * _____

_____

_____

_____

20 __ * _____

_____

_____

_____

20 __ * _____

_____

_____

_____

20 __ * _____

_____

_____

_____

19 DECEMBER

Ask yourself: Whom do I envy? The unpleasant emotion of envy can be a useful clue about changes that you'd like to make in your life.

20 ___ * _____

_____

_____

_____

20 ___ * _____

_____

_____

_____

20 ___ * _____

_____

_____

_____

20 ___ * _____

_____

_____

_____

20 ___ * _____

_____

_____

_____

DECEMBER

"I count him braver who overcomes his desires
than him who conquers his enemies; for the
hardest victory is over self."

—Aristotle

20 __ * _____

_____

_____

_____

20 __ * _____

_____

_____

_____

20 __ * _____

_____

_____

_____

20 __ * _____

_____

_____

_____

20 __ * _____

_____

_____

_____

DECEMBER

"No man knows how bad he is till he has tried very hard to be good. . . . Only those who try to resist temptation know how strong it is."

—*C. S. Lewis*

20 __ * _____

_____

_____

_____

20 __ * _____

_____

_____

_____

20 __ * _____

_____

_____

_____

20 __ * _____

_____

_____

_____

20 __ * _____

_____

_____

_____

DECEMBER

"There is nothing either good or bad,
but thinking makes it so."

—William Shakespeare

20 __ * _____

_____

_____

_____

20 __ * _____

_____

_____

_____

20 __ * _____

_____

_____

_____

20 __ * _____

_____

_____

_____

20 __ * _____

_____

_____

_____

DECEMBER

"If one is the master of one thing and understands one thing well, one has at the same time insight into and understanding of many things."

—*Vincent van Gogh*

20 __ * _____

_____

_____

_____

20 __ * _____

_____

_____

_____

20 __ * _____

_____

_____

_____

20 __ * _____

_____

_____

_____

20 __ * _____

_____

_____

_____

DECEMBER

The sense of smell is a powerful influence over emotions.
Look for ways to add and appreciate pleasant scents, and
to eliminate bad smells from your life.

20 __ * _____

_____

_____

20 __ * _____

_____

_____

20 __ * _____

_____

_____

20 __ * _____

_____

_____

20 __ * _____

_____

_____

DECEMBER

In the tumult of daily life, it can be hard to appreciate the ordinary day, to realize how precious it is, and how fleeting.

20 __ * _____

_____

_____

_____

20 __ * _____

_____

_____

_____

20 __ * _____

_____

_____

_____

20 __ * _____

_____

_____

_____

20 __ * _____

_____

_____

_____

DECEMBER

"The disturbers of happiness are our desires,
our griefs, and our fears."

—*Samuel Johnson*

20 __ * _____

_____

_____

_____

20 __ * _____

_____

_____

_____

20 __ * _____

_____

_____

_____

20 __ * _____

_____

_____

_____

20 __ * _____

_____

_____

_____

27 DECEMBER

"The fact is that very few things have so much effect on the feeling inside a room as the sun shining into it."

—*Christopher Alexander*

20 __ * _____

_____

_____

_____

20 __ * _____

_____

_____

_____

20 __ * _____

_____

_____

_____

20 __ * _____

_____

_____

_____

20 __ * _____

_____

_____

_____

DECEMBER

"What man actually needs is not a tensionless state but rather the striving and struggling for some goal worthy of him. What he needs is not the discharge of tension at any cost, but the call of a potential meaning waiting to be fulfilled by him."

— *Viktor Frankl*

20 __ * _____
_____
_____
_____

20 __ * _____
_____
_____
_____

20 __ * _____
_____
_____
_____

20 __ * _____
_____
_____
_____

20 __ * _____
_____
_____
_____

DECEMBER

Happiness doesn't always make you feel happy.
Often, happiness requires you to do things that
make you feel anxious, resentful, frustrated,
intimidated, or irritable.

20 __ * _____

_____

_____

_____

20 __ * _____

_____

_____

_____

20 __ * _____

_____

_____

_____

20 __ * _____

_____

_____

_____

20 __ * _____

_____

_____

_____

DECEMBER

Be a tourist in your own life. Note your private landmarks,
your important historical sites, your favorite spots.

20 __ *_____

_____

_____

_____

20 __ *_____

_____

_____

_____

20 __ *_____

_____

_____

_____

20 __ *_____

_____

_____

_____

20 __ *_____

_____

_____

_____

31   DECEMBER

"The biggest happiness is when at the end of the year
you feel better than at the beginning."

—*Henry David Thoreau*

20 __ * _____
_____
_____
_____

20 __ * _____
_____
_____
_____

20 __ * _____
_____
_____
_____

20 __ * _____
_____
_____
_____

20 __ * _____
_____
_____
_____